THE
CORONATION
COOKBOOK

Marguerite Patten OBE

hamlyn

First published in Great Britain in 2002 by
Hamlyn, a division of Octopus Publishing
Group Ltd, 2–4 Heron Quays, London E14 4JP

Text copyright © Marguerite Patten 2002
Book design copyright © Octopus Publishing
Group Ltd 2002

ISBN 0 600 60617 1

A CIP catalogue record for this book is available
from the British Library

Printed and bound in China

10 9 8 7 6 5 4 3 2 1

Recipe notes

The following notes will be helpful in following the recipes.

All spoon measures are level. If the word 'level' is included in a recipe it means that it is particularly important to measure that ingredient carefully.
1 tablespoon = one 15 ml spoon
1 teaspoon = one 5 ml spoon
American readers should note that an American tablespoon is smaller than a British one:
1 British tablespoon = 1¼ American tablespoons

Metric and imperial measures are given in all recipes. Use one set only and not a mixture of both. Of course, when most of the dishes were cooked in the earlier part of the 20th century all measurements would have been imperial. Please note that when buying ready packaged food it will often be weighed at 250g not 225g as most of these recipes require.

Eggs should be medium size unless a specific size is indicated. The Department of Health advises that eggs should not be consumed raw. It is prudent for vulnerable people, such as pregnant women and nursing mothers, invalids, the elderly, babies and young children, to avoid dishes containing uncooked or lightly cooked eggs. Once prepared, such dishes should be kept refrigerated and eaten promptly.

Milk should be full fat unless otherwise indicated.

Stock is used in a number of recipes. Do make your own where possible or buy the best quality, ready-prepared stock products.

Fresh herbs should be used wherever possible. If you include dried herbs use half the quantity. A bouquet garni is a small bunch of herbs wrapped in muslin or tied into a bunch with cotton or fine string. Choose the herbs you feel will blend with the dish. Some of the best are basil, bay leaves (use sparingly), celery leaves, chervil, coriander, dill, fennel, parsley (especially flat-leaf parsley), rosemary, savory, tarragon and thyme.

Pepper should be freshly ground black pepper unless stated to the contrary. Use sea salt if possible.

Ovens should be preheated to the temperature indicated. If you are using a fan-assisted oven follow the manufacturer's instructions for adjusting the time and temperature.

Nuts and nut derivatives are used in some dishes in this book. It is essential that people with known allergic reactions to nuts and nut derivatives and those who may be potentially vulnerable to those allergies, such as pregnant women and nursing mothers, invalids, the elderly, babies and children, avoid dishes made with nuts and nut oils. Also, check the labels of ready-prepared ingredients for the possible inclusion of nut derivatives.

Contents

Introduction

The Coronation of British kings and queens is a ceremony of great historical tradition and solemnity. It is an occasion of interest not only to those fortunate enough to attend but also to the population at large, signifying as it does the public avowal by the monarch of the responsibilities of the high office.

In the 20th century there were four coronations, and each was marked by celebrations – both formal and informal – throughout Britain, reflecting the affection and pride with which the population regards the monarchy. This book recaptures some of the grandeur of these coronations, describing both the special royal festivities and the ways in which all sections of the population created their own celebratory events. Two rulers of the last hundred years, George V and Elizabeth II, have also enjoyed jubilees, and these, too, are included here, together with the festive food associated with those occasions.

I have recreated some of the official Coronation menus so that readers can try these at home and enjoy truly royal meals. Because details of the actual recipes for the Coronation and Jubilee dishes are not available, I have interpreted them as I feel they would have been made, but using ingredients that are widely available today.

The dishes in the banquets and special meals reflect the tastes of each particular period, and I have attempted to keep this sense of period, while writing the recipes in such a way that they are easy to reproduce in private kitchens today. In the last five decades, however, our appreciation of different kinds of foods, flavours and textures has increased, and after trying the recipes, you may like to change them slightly. Sauces and gravies, for example, have become less thick in recent years, so use more liquid than given in the recipe or reduce the amount of flour. Herbs such as basil, coriander and flat-leaf parsley are popular today and are easily obtainable, so you should try those instead of the ones that would have been used many years ago.

Although some of the dishes have classic titles, which are easy to identify, many of the names on the menus were intended to honour particular guests at the banquets – Norvégienne, à l'Indienne and so on – and these will not be found in reference books. I have, therefore, tested the recipes with the ingredients that I felt were appropriate.

The dishes prepared for the street parties would have varied in different parts of the country, so I have given some of the most popular dishes of the era.

In each of the reigns covered by this book I have also briefly noted some of the most interesting and important events in Britain and around the world of the year of accession and the Coronation year. This will enable readers to visualize the particular era.

In Britain we are fortunate in having had monarchs who care for the good of their subjects and carry out their high office with grace and dignity. This book is a tribute to the present queen, Elizabeth II, who for so many years has worked so tirelessly and has given the public in Britain and the Commonwealth enormous pride in their royal ruler.

Marguerite Patten

RIGHT: The royal coach passing the Queen Victoria memorial during the Coronation parade in 1937.

History and Regalia

Coronations are solemn ceremonies in which sovereigns are inaugurated into their high office. The earliest recorded coronation in English history occurred in 787, when Ecgfrith was publicly recognized as Offa's successor. The coronation service for the enthronement of Queen Elizabeth II in 1953 derived from that used for King Edgar in Bath in 973, which was, in turn, based on two earlier models, known as the Leofric and Egbert services. The ceremony, therefore, dates from Anglo-Saxon times.

When William of Normandy defeated Harold at the battle of Hastings in 1066 it was stressed that he could not be regarded as king of England until the coronation had taken place at the abbey of Edward the Confessor at Westminster, and Henry I was crowned only a few days after the death of William II to confirm his position. The ceremony continued through the centuries, with that of Elizabeth I on 15 January 1559 being the last to take place in Latin. That of her successor, James I of England and VI of Scotland, on 25 July 1603 was conducted in English.

LEFT: Queen Elizabeth II wearing the State Crown and holding the State Orb in a Royal carriage after her Coronation ceremony.

The ceremony consists of four distinct parts. In the first part, the introduction, the Archbishop of Canterbury presents the sovereign to the company assembled within the cathedral. In the past the sovereign was shown to the people at Westminster Hall and the people were asked if they wanted the service to proceed. This is not done today; instead the sovereign is presented to everyone in the abbey, turning east, south, west and north for the recognition. After this, the archbishop administers the oath.

In the second part, the consecration, the monarch, sitting in the Coronation Chair, is anointed while the choir sings the anthem *Zadok the Priest*. In the third part, the investiture, the anointed sovereign is adorned with symbols of royal power, including the coronation robes, the insignia and the crown. When there is a consort, as in the case of Queens Alexandra, Mary and Elizabeth in the 20th century, their coronation follows at this point.

In part four, the enthronement and homage, the sovereign receives the homage of the Lords Spiritual and Lords Temporal.

For centuries the coronation was followed by a banquet at Westminster Hall, a custom that ended with the coronation of George IV in 1821. During the course of the banquet the king or queen's champion, dressed in full armour, rode into the hall on horseback and threw down his gauntlet three times to challenge anyone to deny the sovereign's right to the crown. The tradition of presenting the gauntlet endures, although the champion no longer wears armour. The king's or queen's champion has the duty of bearing the standard of England during the coronation service.

Coronation regalia

The regalia is kept in the Tower of London, for the items are not only of great historical importance but are, literally, priceless. Much of the original regalia was destroyed by Parliamentarians in 1649, and new pieces had to be created for the coronation of Charles II in 1661. Fortunately, there were records of the older items.

Each part of the regalia plays an essential note in the coronation. The orb and royal sceptre are marks of royalty. The orb is made of gold, decorated with diamonds and pearls; and topped with a cross studded with diamonds, a sapphire and an emerald. The sceptre is made of gold. One end is adorned with diamonds, including the Cullinan diamond, and an amethyst.

St Edward's Crown or Crown of England is the crown used for crowning the monarch in part three of the ceremony. It is gold, set with precious stones. Although it was made for the coronation of Charles II in April 1661, it is named after the crown worn by Edward the Confessor, who was crowned in 1043. The Imperial Crown of State was made for the coronation of Queen Victoria. It contains the Black Prince's ruby, a sapphire from the coronation ring of Edward the Confessor and the diamond known as the Star of India, which was given to Edward VII. This crown is worn by the monarch in the procession at the end of the coronation and on state occasions.

The regalia also includes he Sword of State and other ceremonial swords. The ampulla (a gold flask filled with holy oil) and spoon are used for the consecration and anointing during the service. The spurs and the coronation ring are presented to the monarch during the ceremony.

When a queen consort is crowned another special crown is used. The Imperial Crown of India, which is also housed in the Tower of London, was made especially for the crowning of George V in India in 1911.

EDWARD VII

REIGNED 1901–1910

P RINCE ALBERT EDWARD, THE FIRST SON OF QUEEN VICTORIA AND PRINCE ALBERT, WAS BORN AT BUCKINGHAM PALACE ON 9 NOVEMBER 1841. HIS PARENTS ALREADY HAD A DAUGHTER, PRINCESS VICTORIA (KNOWN AS VICKY), BUT THE BIRTH OF A SON AND HEIR WAS GREETED WITH NATIONAL CELEBRATIONS. THE QUEEN RECORDED THAT HE WAS 'A FINE LARGE BOY', AND WITHIN THE FAMILY HE BECAME KNOWN AS BERTIE. OVER THE YEARS QUEEN VICTORIA'S FAMILY BECAME EXTREMELY LARGE, WITH THE ARRIVAL BETWEEN 1843 AND 1857 OF A FURTHER FOUR DAUGHTERS AND THREE MORE SONS.

Early Years
1841-1863

THE NURSERY ROUTINE FOR THE YOUNG PRINCE WAS STRICT, IN KEEPING WITH THE TRADITIONS OF WEALTHY FAMILIES IN THE 19TH CENTURY. THE ROYAL FAMILY DIVIDED THEIR TIME BETWEEN BUCKINGHAM PALACE, WINDSOR CASTLE AND BALMORAL, THEIR ESTATE IN SCOTLAND, WHICH THEY ACQUIRED IN 1852. THE FAMILY'S MOST INFORMAL TIMES WERE SPENT AT OSBORNE HOUSE ON THE ISLE OF WIGHT, WHICH THEY GENERALLY VISITED IN JULY AND AUGUST. THE QUEEN AND PRINCE ALBERT WERE ABLE TO RELAX THERE, AND THEIR CHILDREN HAD A COMPARATIVELY LIGHT-HEARTED HOLIDAY.

In view of Bertie's position as Prince of Wales and future king, his parents devoted considerable thought to his education. Although this concern was natural, most accounts suggest they tried to overwork the child and rarely, if ever, praised him. Until he went to university he had few opportunities to come into contact with other young people. Instead, he was continually reminded of his important destiny.

When Bertie was barely six years old, his routine, under his governess Miss Hildyard, was amazing. Work started at 8.20 a.m.; he would begin the day with arithmetic, dictation and writing, leading on to French, German, reading, geography and writing. He would then have dancing lessons and more reading. His playtime would be spent on studying a map or counting. In 1849 Henry Birch was appointed tutor to the prince and the young Prince became extremely fond of him. The Queen and Prince Albert, however, expressed their dissatisfaction with the progress made by their son at this time and later in his academic career.

The Prince went to study in Germany in 1857, which not only enhanced his command of the language but added to his love of travel. He had already accompanied his parents on visits to Belgium, and he also joined them on a state visit to Paris to see Emperor Napoleon III and his wife, Eugénie.

In view of their strict control they sought to exercise over their son, it is perhaps surprising that the Queen and Prince Albert arranged for him to have his own residence at White Lodge, Richmond, in 1858, although this certainly did not mean that he could lead an independent life. He continued to be schooled in etiquette and behaviour as well as in academic matters, but his parents still expressed their concern and dissatisfaction with his behaviour. The young Prince was inclined to have sudden attacks of temper, but people close to the royal family felt this was because of the pressures placed on him by his parents, and well-wishers stressed the prince's courtesy towards everyone and his need for affection.

Four terms at Oxford University were interrupted by more travel. He visited his sister Victoria, who was married to Prince Frederick of Prussia, and then went to Rome to broaden his appreciation of art

and to have an audience with the Pope. He also undertook important tours to Canada and the United States, when he represented the Queen, who did not want to endure the long, arduous journey. The Prince travelled throughout Canada to enthusiastic receptions everywhere, and it was stressed that 'he entered into the spirit of the tour', even when the accommodation was rough. He then visited several cities in the United States, where he participated in formal ceremonies and festivities. Throughout the tours he showed confidence and charm, and he received many sincere compliments and congratulations on his conduct.

Even during his time at Oxford University he was denied the opportunity to live in college or ordinary accommodation with other young men, for his father insisted that he should have his own residence. In spite of his semi-isolation, however, he managed to make some friends. He then went to Cambridge, again living in his own private residence. His time at university appears to have increased his delight in the theatre and to have awakened a desire to spend some time in the army.

In 1861 he was given the opportunity to experience military training when he spent the long vacation with the infantry in Ireland. He was awarded the rank of lieutenant-colonel. The military programme outlined for the Prince by his father was far too demanding, and he was unable to fulfil it satisfactorily. This

ABOVE: Prince Edward, who in his younger years studied at Cambridge and then went on to begin military training in Ireland.

angered his parents, and their distress was intensified by the Prince's association with an actress. When the young Prince returned to Cambridge from Ireland his father visited him to reproach him for the liaison. Prince Albert was unwell at the time. It was not realized that he was suffering from typhoid.

Prince Albert died at Windsor Castle on 14 December 1861. Queen Victoria always attributed his premature death to the Prince of Wales, for she felt that if he had not gone to Cambridge while he was unwell, he might have recovered.

Marriage

1863

LEFT: Prince Edward and his bride Princess Alexandra of Denmark just after their marriage, posing with Queen Victoria.

AFTER THE DEATH OF PRINCE ALBERT THE QUEEN TRIED TO CARRY OUT HER VARIOUS DUTIES EXACTLY AS SHE FELT THE PRINCE CONSORT WOULD HAVE WISHED. THEY HAD DECIDED THAT AN EARLY MARRIAGE FOR THE PRINCE OF WALES WAS DESIRABLE, AND THEY HAD CONSIDERED VARIOUS ELIGIBLE LADIES. THE PRINCE HAD STATED THAT HE WANTED TO MARRY SOMEONE WITH WHOM HE WAS GENUINELY IN LOVE, AND THE LADY CHOSEN WAS PRINCESS ALEXANDRA OF DENMARK.

The wedding was celebrated at St George's Chapel, Windsor, on 10 March 1863, after which the Prince and Princess of Wales honeymooned for just one week at Osborne House. As the wedding was not held in London the engaged couple travelled through the city streets when the prince escorted his bride-to-be from Gravesend. People were enchanted by the vivacious and beautiful princess.

The London home of the Prince and Princess of Wales was Marlborough House, which underwent some much-needed renovations, and their country home was the recently purchased Sandringham in Norfolk, where the Prince enjoyed shooting.

After the death of Prince Albert, Queen Victoria was unwilling to participate in social events, and the Prince and Princess fulfilled these duties with grace and charm. Their family life began in January 1864 with the birth of an heir, Albert Victor, to be followed within a period of six years by five more children, although sadly one son died within hours of his birth. The parents were delighted with their family, and there was far less of the strict discipline of the Victorian nursery. The Prince of Wales might shout at people who displeased him, but he never raised his voice at his children.

In addition to official social events, Edward began his own round of pleasure,

ABOVE: **A photographic record of the meeting of Prince Edward's family and the family of his Danish wife the day before their wedding.**

visiting friends and the theatre and participating in after-theatre parties with enthusiasm. He entertained a great deal at Sandringham, although his London life appealed more. In 1870 he was involved as a witness in a divorce case, although he was not directly implicated, and this so shocked the public that the Prince and Princess were booed at the theatre.

Edward also travelled abroad, often visiting his relations at the various courts of Europe. After much discussion, he visited India in the winter of 1875–6, although he was disappointed that Alexandra was not permitted to go with him. It was felt necessary that a member of the royal family should visit the subcontinent because there had been considerable unrest there. Edward, with a large group of friends and advisers, went

as a guest of the Viceroy. He travelled widely and gained a reputation for the courtesy he showed to everyone he met and for his ability to cope with the heat. He was also able to indulge his passion for shooting wild animals.

The Prince of Wales's liaisons with various women are well known, but far less publicized was his ability to get on with people of all classes and his shrewd grasp of world and national affairs. His mother excluded him from any official place in government business.

Queen Alexandra
1844-1925

QUEEN ALEXANDRA WAS BLESSED IN THAT ALL HER CHILDREN ADORED HER. SHE RETURNED THEIR LOVE, BOTH IN PERSON AND IN LETTERS. EVEN WHEN GEORGIE, HER SECOND SON (WHO LATER BECAME KING GEORGE V), WAS AN ADULT NAVAL OFFICER, SHE WROTE TO HIM 'A GREAT BIG KISS FOR YOUR LOVELY LITTLE FACE'. BERTIE'S SISTER VICTORIA DESCRIBED HER AS 'ONE OF THE MOST LADY-LIKE AND ARISTOCRATIC-LOOKING PEOPLE I HAVE EVER SEEN.'

RIGHT: Queen Alexandra at Mar Lodge, *circa* 1904.
FAR RIGHT: The King and Queen on a leisurely stroll in their grounds during their reign.

Queen Alexandra had one serious failing: she was consistently unpunctual for events. This annoyed Edward, but he still admired and loved his wife, and it certainly did not diminish Alexandra's charm and vivacity, which was so enjoyed by her family, her friends and the British people. In turn, she must have had an exceptional love for her husband to accept the fact that he had mistresses, even inviting one of them, Mrs Keppel, to visit him when it was known that he was dying.

Like Edward, Alexandra was related to many of the ruling houses of Europe. Her father ascended to the throne of Denmark in 1863 as Christian IX, and her mother was Princess Louise of Hesse-Cassel. Her younger sister, Dagmar, married the prince who became Tsar Alexander III of Russia, and her younger brother, George, became king of the Hellenes. Princess Maud, one of the daughters of Edward VII and Alexandra, married a prince of Denmark, who was subsequently elected king of Norway as Haakon VII.

Queen Alexandra travelled less widely than Edward, but on the occasions she went abroad without him he always met her at Victoria Station. One of the few times he missed doing so was immediately before his death, when he was too ill.

The Queen did a great deal for hospitals. In 1902 she founded the Queen Alexandra Imperial Military Nursing Service, and in 1912 she instituted Alexandra Rose Day to

raise funds for hospitals. The King admitted the Queen to the Order of the Garter, a rare honour, for no women had been admitted since Tudor times.

The King and Queen enjoyed the company of their children and grandchildren, and when the Prince and Princess of Wales went to India the royal grandparents

looked after their grandchildren at Sandringham.

After Edward VII's death Marlborough House became Queen Alexandra's official home, but she spent much of her time at Sandringham with her unmarried daughter, Victoria. She died in November 1925 and was buried at Windsor.

Accession and After

1901

LEFT: The funeral cortege of Queen Victoria (1819–1901) leaving Windsor Castle for the mausoleum at Frogmore.

WHEN QUEEN VICTORIA DIED THE NEWSPAPERS CARRIED HEADLINES SUCH AS 'QUEEN VICTORIA DIES; AN ERA ENDS'. EDWARD VII APPROACHED THE UPBRINGING OF HIS CHILDREN VERY DIFFERENTLY FROM HIS OWN CHILDHOOD. HE WAS AFFECTIONATE AND INDULGENT, ENJOYING HIS CHILDREN'S COMPANY AND MAKING NO GREAT DEMANDS ON THEIR ACADEMIC PROWESS. THEIR MOTHER SHOWED MUCH LOVE TO HER FAMILY BUT INSISTED THAT THEY HAD A COMPARATIVELY SIMPLE LIFESTYLE AND DID NOT BECOME OVERBEARING OR PROUD.

In Paris chauffeurs protest at a move to stop them wearing moustaches.

July

British-occupied parts of Beijing (Peking) are handed back to the Chinese authorities.

In New York nearly 400 people die in one day when temperatures reach up to 43.3°C (110°F) in the shade.

In France the speed limit for cars is set at 10 km (6¼ miles) an hour.

August

The House of Commons votes an extra £12.5 million for the naval and war budgets.

In South Africa Lord Kitchener tells the Boers that they must surrender by 15 September or face banishment; they ignore him.

The Empress Victoria of Germany, mother of Kaiser Wilhelm II and eldest child of Queen Victoria, dies.

In Detroit, Michigan, a motorcar company is named after the 18th-century explorer Antoine de la Mothe Cadillac.

September

In Buffalo, New York, President McKinley is fatally wounded by a Polish anarchist; Vice-President Roosevelt becomes president.

The Boxer Rising ends when the Allies finally sign a peace protocol with the Chinese.

Henri Toulouse-Lautrec, the French painter, dies aged 36.

An outbreak of smallpox spreads in London.

October

Britain's first submarine (petrol driven) is launched at Barrow-in-Furness by Vickers, with plans for four more.

General Louis Botha's forces inflict heavy losses on British soldiers at Brakenlaagte.

President Roosevelt invites Booker T. Washington, the black reformer, teacher and head of the first university for coloured people, to dinner at the White House, leading to race riots in which 34 people die.

November

A second Hay-Pauncefote treaty agrees the building of the Panama Canal, giving the USA extensive rights in return for a guarantee of the canal's neutrality.

A new telephone system for London is completed.

December

In Sweden the first Nobel prizes are awarded: for physics to Wilhelm Röntgen, for chemistry to J. H. van't Hoff, for medicine to Emil von Behring and for literature to Sully Prudhomme.

Radio signals transmitted from Poldhu, Cornwall, are received in Newfoundland over 3,200 km (2,000 miles) away.

David Lloyd George is prevented from speaking in Birmingham by anti-Boer protesters.

A woman doctor in Macclesfield resigns when male colleagues refuse to work with her because of her sex.

ABOVE: William McKinley is inaugurated as the 25th President of the United States. He is seen here making his 'What a mighty power for good is a united nation' speech in Memphis, Tennessee.

Events of 1902

ABOVE: Beatrix Potter (1866–1943), the British author and illustrator of children's books, has her first book, *The Tale of Peter Rabbit*, published during this year.

January

Smallpox affects more than 2,000 people in London, and special quarantine ships and reception centres are requisitioned.

Malta adopts English, rather than Italian, as her official language.

For the first time a French soccer team plays in England; Marlow FC defeats Paris 4–0.

February

England scores 769 runs in a single test innings in Australia.

In London women workers demanding votes for women present a petition bearing 37,000 signatures to Parliament.

March

Cecil Rhodes dies at the age of 48 and is buried, as he wished, in Rhodesia.

British soldiers are allowed to wear spectacles on or off duty.

In Italy the minimum working age is raised from 9 to 12 for boys and from 11 to 15 for girls.

In South Africa more than 900 Boers are killed or captured.

April

Sir Henry Irving takes the leading role in *Faust* at the Lyceum Theatre, London.

A fire destroys large parts of the Barbican in London.

In Britain the Budget puts 1d on income tax and 2d duty on cheques and raises grain duties.

Cecil Rhodes leaves £6 million to fund scholarships to Oxford University for students from the British Empire, the USA and Germany.

May

The treaty of Vereeniging ends the war in South Africa, the Boers accepting British sovereignty.

The aviator August Severs dies when his airship explodes over Paris.

In Germany the government denies the right to women to form political associations.

In Paris audiences are entertained by the first moving pictures, Georges Méliès's *Le Voyage dans la lune*.

June

Sarah Bernhardt, who had first appeared on the London stage over 20 years ago, triumphs in her best known role in *La Dame aux camélias*.

Russia imposes Russian as the official language in Finland.

The United States pays $40 million for a French company's concession to build the Panama Canal, which will shorten the distance between the US coasts by 12,870 km (8,000 miles).

July

Arthur James Balfour becomes Prime Minister on Lord Salisbury's retirement.

Eight Bills for the building of the London Underground receive their second reading.

A French Renault wins the first Paris–Vienna race.

In Venice the Campanile of St Mark's Cathedral, 99 m (322 ft) high, collapses.

An international conference dedicated to the suppression of white slavery opens in Paris.

August

The Shah of Persia begins a visit to Britain.

The General Post Office and American Express Company agree to carry parcels between Britain and the USA.

The Imperial Vaccination League is formed in London to eradicate smallpox.

In Belfast Harland & Wolff launch the 21,000-ton *Cedric*, the world's largest liner.

September

The Automobile Club organizes trials from the Crystal Palace in London to Folkestone and back to show that cars are almost as reliable as railways as a means of transport. 63 cars take part.

In Dublin, Ireland, 20,000 people demonstrate against Britain's strict measures to keep order during the state of emergency.

In South Africa 15,000 applications for gold-mining licenses are received in a single week.

The nationalist German Union of the Eastern Marshes meets in Danzig to demand harsher measures to suppress Polish culture and language.

October

In Egypt it is reported that 32,000 people have died from cholera.

It is announced that Windsor Castle will be open to the public when the court is absent.

Theodore Roosevelt settles the five-month-old coal strike in Pennsylvania by appointing a commission to investigate the miners' claims.

In France two-thirds of all miners are on strike.

November

Lord Tennyson, the son of the Victorian poet, is appointed Governor-General of Australia for one year.

J.M. Barrie's *The Admirable Crichton* is premiered at the Criterion Theatre, London.

Kaiser William II begins a 12-day visit to Britain to try to improve Anglo-German relations.

In Paris the first professional photography conference opens.

December

Beatrix Potter's first book, *The Tale of Peter Rabbit*, illustrated by the author, is published.

In Egypt the massive Aswan dam, 790 km (490 miles) south of Cairo, opens, after four years of construction by a work force of 11,000.

Ronald Ross, a British army doctor, wins the Nobel prize for medicine for his work on the causes of malaria.

Marconi sends the first transatlantic telegraph message from Canada to King Edward VII in London.

ABOVE: Portrait of the Imperialist, Cecil John Rhodes (1853–1902) who left £6 million to fund scholarships to Oxford University.

Coronation Year
1902

ABOVE: A ticket to Westminster Abbey for the Coronation of King Edward VII.

THE CORONATION WAS PLANNED FOR 26 JUNE 1902, AND AS THE DATE DREW NEAR EXCITEMENT MOUNTED. THE WAR IN SOUTH AFRICA HAD ENDED WITH THE DEFEAT OF THE BOERS, SO BRITAIN FELT IT COULD ENJOY THE CELEBRATIONS THAT WERE AHEAD. LONDON WAS DECKED WITH FLAGS AND BUNTING, AND IT WAS PLANNED THAT FRESH FLOWERS WOULD BE PLACED ALONG THE ROUTE AT THE LAST MINUTE. VISITORS FROM THE ROYAL FAMILIES OF EUROPE, AND REPRESENTATIVES OF GOVERNMENTS FROM AROUND THE WORLD AND FROM THE EMPIRE WERE CONVERGING ON THE CAPITAL.

On 23 June Edward arrived at Buckingham Palace from Windsor Castle. He was ill and in pain, but with the Coronation imminent the illness was at first kept secret. However, his doctors insisted that he had acute appendicitis, with the possibility of a burst appendix, and that they must operate. The Coronation would have to be postponed. He was operated on at Buckingham Palace on 24 June. When it became known that he had successfully survived such a serious illness, there was great rejoicing. Edward VII had already become a popular monarch.

The new date chosen for the Coronation was 9 August, and the King spent his convalescence aboard the royal yacht *Victoria and Albert*. Because he might not have been able to walk in his usual brisk style a ramp was to be erected at the abbey, and plans were made to have a slightly shorter service than usual.

MEAL FOR 450,000

In July 1902 the King and Queen treated the poor of London to dinner with music and singing to celebrate his Coronation. It was estimated that 450,000 sat down to eat, and the meals took place at 700 venues. It cost the King £30,000 with contributions from others, notably the brewers, while barristers rolled up their sleeves and washed the potatoes. More than 1,500 entertainers were booked, and pianists moved from place to place and gave their services free. Everywhere buildings were decorated and Covent Garden was bedecked with flowers.

In 1902 cooking facilities were limited. Ovens were not standard equipment on every coal range, and gas and electric cookers were a rarity, so it was important that the chosen main course could be cooked in an oven or a very large pan on top of the cookers. Doubtless the choice of dishes would vary from place to place.

As a lover of good food, King Edward would approve of a dish created by the great chef of the era, Auguste Escoffier, and I have chosen his *Carbonnade Flamande* as a representative dish, for meat would be a treat for the poor at the time. The pudding is a lighter version of a Christmas pudding, generally referred to as 'plum pudding' in those days.

ABOVE: Prince Edward wearing state robes for his Coronation.

MENU
FLEMISH CARBONNADE OF BEEF, ACCOMPANIED BY CREAMED
POTATOES AND CARROTS
ORANGE PLUM PUDDING WITH CUSTARD SAUCE

FLEMISH CARBONNADE OF BEEF

The inclusion of beer in this recipe was appropriate because brewers were among the people who aided the King and Queen by donations to their cause. To balance the slightly bitter flavour given by beer, sugar is included, as indicated in the recipe; the amount can be varied to suit personal taste. Prepare the beurre manie first, so it is ready to thicken the sauce.

PREPARATION TIME: 30 MINUTES

COOKING TIME: 2 HOURS 40 MINUTES

SERVES: 4–6

Beurre manie

40 g (1½ oz) butter

40 g (1½ oz) plain flour

Carbonnade

750–875 g (1½–1¾ lb) lean, good quality stewing steak, thinly sliced

50 g (2 oz) butter*

1 tablespoon sunflower oil*

4–5 large onions, thinly sliced

600 ml (1 pint) beer

300 ml (½ pint) stock, preferably beef

bouquet garni

1–1½ tablespoons brown sugar, or to taste

salt and pepper

*Butter and oil would be a modern choice and these could have been chosen on the Continent, even in the time of Edward VII. Grand chefs may have used butter and oil but cooks would undoubtedly have used all dripping or all lard when this dish was made to celebrate the Coronation of Edward VII.

Make the beurre manie by creaming the butter and flour together.

To make the carbonnade, season the meat with a generous amount of salt and pepper just before cooking. Heat half the butter and half the oil in a large saucepan, add the meat and cook for 1 minute on either side; remove from the pan on to a plate.

Heat the remaining butter and oil in the same pan, add the onions and cook steadily until golden.

Put layers of meat and onions into a casserole. Add the beer and stock to the pan; stir briskly to absorb the meat juices. When boiling, add small pieces of beurre manie until the desired consistency is achieved. Add the bouquet garni and sugar. Pour the mixture into the casserole, cover tightly and cook in a preheated oven, 150°C (300°F), Gas Mark 2, for 2½ hours.

Remove the bouquet garni. Serve the carbonnade from the casserole with creamed potatoes and cooked carrots.

Variation

The carbonnade can be cooked in a saucepan over a low heat. Thicken with the beurre manie just before serving so that the sauce does not stick to the pan. Check throughout the cooking period that there is sufficient liquid in the pan.

ORANGE PLUM PUDDING

Shredded suet is used in this recipe, but it can be replaced by melted butter or margarine. When this pudding was made in the early decades of the 20th century it would have been covered with a floured cloth instead of greaseproof paper and foil, which we use today. The raisins available in the 1900s would have been large and would have needed stoning and chopping before they were added to the mix. If you use marmalade containing large pieces of peel, chop them before adding them to the other ingredients. Custard powder was well known at this period, and the custard served with the pudding would be made with that.

PREPARATION TIME: 25 MINUTES PLUS 1 HOUR TO SOAK DRIED FRUIT

COOKING TIME: 2 HOURS

SERVES: 6–8

100 g (3½ oz) raisins

100 g (3½ oz) sultanas

100 g (3½ oz) currants

6 tablespoons beer (preferably a light lager type) or extra orange juice

2 tablespoons orange juice

100 g (3½ oz) crystallized orange peel, finely chopped

50 g (2 oz) blanched almonds, finely chopped

150 g (5 oz) suet, shredded or finely chopped (use meat or vegetarian type)

150 g (5 oz) soft brown sugar

2 tablespoons orange marmalade

2 teaspoons grated orange rind

150 g (5 oz) soft breadcrumbs

100 g (3½ oz) self-raising flour or plain flour with 1 teaspoon baking powder

1 small dessert apple, peeled and grated

2 eggs, beaten

Put the dried fruit into a basin. Cover with the beer (if you are using this) and orange juice and leave for 1 hour.

Mix the fruit, and any liquid which has not been absorbed, with the other ingredients. Spoon into a 1.8 litre (3 pint) greased basin. Cover well and place in a steamer.

Allow the water under the steamer to boil steadily for the first hour. The heat can be turned down so that it simmers gently for the remaining hour.

Turn out the pudding and serve hot with custard sauce.

For Children

It is not stated if special dishes were made for children, and I am therefore assuming they would partake of the dishes above.

THE CORONATION OF EDWARD VII

In August the Coronation went ahead after the delay caused by the King's illness. The streets of London were again decked with the panoply of celebration, for the King had made it clear that he wanted the Coronation to be a time of great pomp, ceremony and colour, and there were flowers and flags everywhere.

The peeresses wore their most magnificent gowns, studded with diamonds, and as the processions passed there were particular cheers for Sir Alfred Gaselee, who had led British troops in China, and for Lord Kitchener, who had triumphed in South Africa. There was special admiration for beautiful Queen Alexandra, and the King was greeted with huge enthusiasm.

Inside Westminster Abbey the ramp provided proved unnecessary as the King appeared in good health, although he did not carry the heavy Sword of State to the altar nor walk to the four points of the compass, as is usual, nor were his two nurses called upon to give any medical treatment. They had been accommodated in a gallery above the coronation chair, each equipped with medicines in case they were needed. It was, in fact, the Archbishop of Canterbury who appeared unwell, not the King, who acquitted himself with the dignity demanded of the occasion.

Opposite is a copy of the menu for the banquet held at Buckingham Palace on 23 June, prior to the original date planned for the Coronation on 26 June 1902. Even though the King was too ill to attend this banquet, the guests were already in London, and so it took place.

BUCKINGHAM PALACE BANQUET

◇

Consommé Printanier à l'Impériale
Consommé Froid à l'Indienne

◇

Blanchailles au Naturel et à la Diable
Filets de Truites à la Russe

◇

Côtelettes de Cailles à la Clamart
Poulardes à la Norvégienne

◇

Selles de Présalé à la Niçoise
Jambon d'Espagne à la Basque

◇

Ortolans Rôtis sur Canapés
Salade de Quatre Saisons
Asperges Froides à la Vinaigrette

◇

Gâteau Punch Granit au Champagne
Gradins de Pâtisseries

◇

Canapés d'Anchois à la Provençale

◇

Petits Soufflés Glacés Princesse
Gauffrettes

CONSOMMÉ PRINTANIER À L'IMPÉRIALE
IMPERIAL CHICKEN CONSOMMÉ

Consommé printanier is a clear soup based on chicken consommé (see page 89). The garnishes are strips of young, new season carrots or turnips, which should be lightly cooked in the consommé. Fresh peas and finely diced French beans should be lightly cooked in well-seasoned stock then added to the soup, which is finally garnished with tiny squares of lettuce and chervil leaves. The addition of the words *à l'Impériale* **is in honour of the great occasion.**

CONSOMMÉ FROID À L'INDIENNE
CHILLED MULLIGATAWNY

The clear mulligatawny soup is served either chilled or very lightly iced. The onions and garlic do not need to be finely chopped because the soup is strained.

PREPARATION TIME: 40 MINUTES PLUS TIME TO CHILL THE SOUP

COOKING TIME: 1½ HOURS PLUS TIME TO MAKE STOCK

SERVES: 6–8

50 g (2 oz) butter
1½–2 teaspoons curry powder, or to taste
3 medium onions, chopped
2–3 garlic cloves, chopped
1 tablespoon lemon juice
1.2 litres (2 pints) well-flavoured beef or mutton stock
2 tablespoons raisins
2 tablespoons grated apple
salt and pepper
To garnish
lemon twists
fresh coriander

Heat the butter in a saucepan, stir in the curry powder, then add the onions and cook for 3 minutes. Add the garlic and all the remaining ingredients, cover tightly and simmer for nearly 1½ hours, season to taste with salt and pepper.

Cool, so that any fat settles on top of the soup; remove this, then reheat the soup and strain through fine gauze to give a clear liquid.

Chill thoroughly or freeze very lightly, then serve in chilled soup cups.. Garnish with twists of lemon and fresh coriander.

BLANCHAILLES AU NATUREL
FRIED WHITEBAIT

Coat whitebait with a little seasoned flour and shallow or deep fry in hot oil or lard (the latter would be used at this time in most homes). Drain well on kitchen paper and season with salt and pepper. Garnish with sprigs of deep-fried parsley.

Fried fish or other fried foods would be served on damask table napkins or dish papers (plain doilies).

BLANCHAILLES À LA DIABLE
DEVILLED WHITEBAIT

Cook the whitebait as above and serve sprinkled with salt and a very little curry powder. To obtain an even coating of curry powder it should be put into a shaker with a very fine hole.

FILETS DE TRUITES À LA RUSSE

TROUT À LA RUSSE

This classic dish can be made with whole or filleted trout. The fish is poached in a court bouillon then coated with hollandaise sauce (also known as Dutch sauce). The Russian touch is given by the garnish of caviar. Some variations give a thick cream topping rather than the sauce (see Variations).

PREPARATION TIME: 35 MINUTES

COOKING TIME: 40 MINUTES

SERVES: 4

8 trout fillets

Hollandaise Sauce (see page 35)

caviar

Court bouillon

600 ml (1 pint) white wine

1 small onion, chopped

1 carrot, chopped

1 sprig of thyme

1 sprig of rosemary

salt and pepper

To garnish

lemon slices

parsley

Make the court bouillon. Bring the liquid and the other ingredients to the boil, lower the heat, cover the pan and simmer for 30 minutes. Strain and return to the pan. Put in the fish and simmer for 10 minutes or until tender. Lift out carefully and arrange on a heated dish.

Coat with warm hollandaise sauce and top with a small amount of caviar. Garnish and serve.

Variations

Blend a little lemon juice and salt and pepper into 225 ml (7½ fl oz) whipped double cream and coat the fish with this.

Instead of court bouillon, cook the fish in water, with a little salt and pepper and a good squeeze of lemon juice.

Mock caviar can be purchased quite inexpensively.

CÔTELETTES DE CAILLES À LA CLAMART

QUAIL WITH ARTICHOKE HEARTS

Quail were one of the popular small game birds at the beginning of the 20th century, and they are readily available today. Choose really plump birds. In this dish only the breasts are used; the legs and carcass make good stock. *A la clamart* is not a usual garnish for quail but I have interpreted it as using artichoke hearts, which is a classic way of serving the birds.

PREPARATION TIME: 45 MINUTES

COOKING TIME: 35 MINUTES AND 1 HOUR FOR THE STOCK

SERVES: 4

8 quail

1.2 litres (2 pints) water

1 onion, chopped

1 large tomato, chopped

50 g (2 oz) mushrooms, sliced

25 g (1 oz) plain flour

50 g (2 oz) butter

4 tablespoons Madeira wine

1 tablespoon redcurrant jelly

4 cooked or canned artichoke hearts

salt and pepper

lettuce, to garnish

Cut the breasts from the quail and put them on one side. Place the rest of the birds in a pan with the water, onion, tomato and mushrooms and season with salt and pepper. Bring the liquid to the boil, cover the pan then simmer for 1 hour. Strain the stock; if necessary return to the pan and boil briskly until 450 ml (¾ pint) remains.

Coat the quail breasts with seasoned flour. Heat the butter in a pan, add the quail and fry gently until golden in colour. Pour in nearly all the stock and simmer for 15 minutes or until the birds are tender and the sauce has thickened. Add the Madeira with the redcurrant jelly. Heat gently and adjust the seasoning.

Heat the last of the stock and warm the artichoke hearts, drain these and arrange on hot plates. Top with the quail and the sauce, then garnish and serve.

Lettuces

No mention is made of the type of lettuce used in salads or for garnishes. This would have varied according to what was available. It is only in modern times that there has been such variety and emphasis on choosing a particular type of lettuce.

POULARDES À LA NORVÉGIENNE

CHICKEN À LA NORVÉGIENNE

The word 'poularde' was used extensively in the past to describe a large **Surrey fowl**, one of the most sought-after chickens. At the beginning of the 20th century the bird would be roasted in the oven or on a turning spit over the heat or simmered in a good white stock. It is interesting to note that some recipes suggest 'barding' (inserting fat bacon or pork strips into the breast) to keep it moist. **Surrey fowl are not widely known today; use an organic bird instead.**

A la Norvégienne is the name of the salad accompaniment served with hot or cold chicken.

PREPARATION TIME: 30 MINUTES

COOKING TIME: SEE METHOD

SERVES: 4–6

1 small organic* chicken, approximately 2 kg (4 lb)

50 g (2 oz) butter or 2 tablespoons olive oil

salt and pepper

Norvégienne salad

175 g (6 oz) cooked new potatoes

175 g (6 oz) cooked prime beef

150 g (5 oz) smoked herrings

1 medium cooked beetroot, skinned

1 medium dessert apple, peeled and cored

Vinaigrette Dressing (see page 34)

*All poultry of this era would be fed on natural foods and be free range so could be described as 'organic'.

Weigh the chicken. Spread just over half the butter or oil over the bird, put the rest inside and season lightly. For a prime bird, roast in a preheated oven, 200°C (400°F), Gas Mark 6, allowing 15 minutes per 450 g (1 lb) and 15 minutes over, but check carefully during the cooking time because modern poultry is very young and tender and overcooking spoils the texture. To test if the chicken is cooked, insert the tip of a sharp knife where the leg joins the body. Any juice that runs out should be clear; if it is slightly pink the bird is not cooked.

To make the salad, dice all the ingredients and mix them together with a little dressing. Serve slices of hot or cold chicken beside the colourful salad.

Variations

Canned anchovy fillets are sometimes added to the salad.

When smoked herring is not available use well-drained rollmop herrings.

SELLES DE PRÉSALÉ À LA NIÇOISE

SADDLE OF MUTTON WITH SALAD NIÇOISE

The word 'présalé' is usually given as 'Pré-Salé', and it refers to mutton, which was readily available in the early part of the 20th century. Salad Niçoise indicates that the meat may have been served cold. Salad Niçoise was a classic dish at the time but was slightly different from the modern version. Today cooked lamb would probably be offered instead of mutton.

PREPARATION TIME: 30 MINUTES

COOKING TIME: 30 MINUTES PLUS TIME TO COOK MUTTON

SERVES: 4–6

cooked lamb or mutton

Salad Niçoise

225 g (8 oz) cooked new potatoes, peeled or scrubbed

175 g (6 oz) cooked French or green beans

2–3 medium tomatoes, skinned

8–12 black olives, stoned and quartered

50 g (2 oz) canned anchovy fillets, drained and chopped

1 tablespoon chopped capers

½ small lettuce heart, shredded

Vinaigrette Dressing (see page 34)

To make the Salad Niçoise, neatly and evenly dice the potatoes and beans; halve the tomatoes, remove the seeds then cut the pulp into thin strips. Mix together the potatoes, beans, tomatoes, olives, anchovies and capers.

Spoon the salad on to a bed of lettuce and place in the centre of the dish. Top with the dressing just before serving. Arrange thin slices of meat around the edge of the salad.

JAMBON D'ESPAGNE À LA BASQUE
SPANISH HAM À LA BASQUE

Spanish hams are mild and sweet in flavour, the best coming from Asturias. The dish is a simple one: the cooked ham is served with garlic-flavoured peas, which indicates that the ham was served hot for the banquet.

Prime gammon could be used instead of the Spanish ham. Modern, sweet-cured gammon does not require soaking before cooking, but if you like a very mild flavour soak the ham for several hours in cold water, then discard the water.

Place the gammon in a pan with water to cover. Vegetables, such as onions, carrots and chopped celery, could be added for additional flavour, as well as ground pepper or a few peppercorns.

Bring the water to the boil, then lower the heat, cover the pan and simmer. Allow 20 minutes per 450 g (1 lb) from the time the water reaches boiling point.

Cook the peas, allowing 3 garlic cloves to each 450 g (1 lb) peas. Heat 25 g (1 oz) butter in a saucepan, add the garlic and heat gently for 2–3 minutes. Meanwhile, cook the peas in water in the usual way, strain and add to the garlic. Mix well then season to taste.

ORTOLANS RÔTIS SUR CANAPÉS
ROAST ORTOLAN CANAPÉS

Ortolans are a type of bunting, formerly regarded as a delicacy. Escoffier wrote of these small birds dismissively: 'The ortolan has no real gastronomic value unless it is roasted and eaten as soon as cooked.' He then suggested they should be wrapped in vine leaves and served on a small cushion of crisp flaky pastry, and topped with foie gras, and this might have been the way the birds were served at the Coronation banquet of 1902. They have become a taste of the past and are difficult to obtain in Britain.

Larousse has an entirely different opinion of the birds, noting that 'they enjoy a high reputation as a table delicacy'.

Salade de Quatre Saisons
Four Seasons Salad

There is no classic recipe for this salad, but its name suggests that you should select ingredients that come from spring, summer, autumn and winter. The salad would be served in a Vinaigrette Dressing (see page 34).

ASPERGES FROIDES À LA VINAIGRETTE

CHILLED ASPARAGUS À LA VINAIGRETTE

The ideal way to cook asparagus is to stand the washed stems in an asparagus basket and place this in boiling salted water. If a basket is not available gently tie bunches of 6–8 stems with fine string to keep them upright in a deep saucepan of boiling water.

At the time of the banquet, taste would have determined that the cooked asparagus would be tender and firm, but not limp. Today we prefer it crisp, and cooking times would be appreciably shorter. In the past the timing for cooking thick stems in boiling salted water was 18–20 minutes; if you are cooking asparagus today allow about half that time or even a little less if you are serving it cold because the vegetable continues to cook slightly as it cools.

If you do not possess a really deep saucepan lay the asparagus flat in a small quantity of boiling salted water, cover and simmer as above.

To serve, place about 6 stems on individual plates and serve the vinaigrette dressing separately or simply spoon 2–3 tablespoons of the dressing on to each plate.

Vinaigrette Dressing

This is the classic way of making this dressing which dates back through the centuries. In the past it was called 'French dressing'.

PREPARATION TIME: 5 MINUTES

SERVES: 4

½ –1 teaspoon made English mustard or French mustard
good pinch of sugar, or to taste
5 tablespoons extra virgin olive oil
2½ tablespoons white or red wine vinegar, or to taste
salt and pepper

Blend the mustard, salt and pepper, sugar and oil then gradually whisk in the vinegar.

Variations

Dressings for salads have altered a great deal. While virgin olive oil is recognized as the finest to use, it is a little heavy for some salads, and other oils, such as sunflower, groundnut or nut oils, can be used.

The range of vinegars available has also increased. If you wish, try a little sherry vinegar, or balsamic or cider vinegar or rice vinegar. Alternatively, lemon juice could be used instead of vinegar.

Oils

Oil was a form of fat not used by the average British cook. It was not sold by grocers but by chemists, so was regarded as a health ingredient, rather than a culinary one. It must be remembered however that the chefs who worked at Buckingham Palace and other royal residences would have known about them, from their training and experience of working on the Continent and undoubtedly they would have used these oils in many of the dishes they prepared

Hollandaise Sauce

PREPARATION TIME: 10 MINUTES

COOKING TIME: 6–7 MINUTES

SERVES: 4

175 g (6 oz) butter

3 egg yolks

shake of cayenne pepper (optional)

2 tablespoons lemon juice or white wine vinegar, or to taste

salt and pepper

Cut the butter into small pieces and leave it at room temperature. Put the egg yolks, cayenne, salt and pepper and most of the lemon juice or vinegar into the top of a double saucepan or basin over hot, but not boiling, water. Whisk over the heat until the mixture thickens, then gradually whisk in the butter. Taste and adjust the seasoning and the amount of lemon juice or vinegar.

Variation

For modern tastes the amount of butter could be reduced.

GÂTEAU PUNCH
FRUIT AND WINE JELLY

The Victorians and Edwardians were extremely fond of alcohol-flavoured jellies, and this gâteau is a delicious fruit-filled wine jelly. The weight of the fruit means you must be generous with the gelatine.

PREPARATION TIME: 20 MINUTES PLUS TIME FOR SETTING

COOKING TIME: A FEW MINUTES

SERVES: 6

150 ml (¼ pint) water

50 g (2 oz) caster sugar

strip of lemon rind

1½ sachets powder gelatine or leaf gelatine to set 900 ml (1½ pints)

600 ml (1 pint) Sauternes or other sweet white wine

2 tablespoons brandy

100 g (3½ oz) raspberries

100 g (3½ oz) small alpine strawberries

Put the water, sugar and lemon rind into a saucepan. Stir until the sugar has dissolved. Soften the gelatine in 150 ml (¼ pint) of the cold wine. Add the remainder of the wine to the saucepan and heat gently, but do not boil. Stir in the gelatine and the wine in which it was soaked.

Heat gently until the gelatine has dissolved then add the brandy and remove the lemon rind. Spoon about one-third of the jelly into a mould and chill until set. Allow the rest of the jelly to remain at room temperature so that it becomes cool but does not set. Arrange half the raspberries and strawberries over the set jelly. Spoon in half the remaining jelly and chill until set.

Add a final layer of fruit and the last of the jelly. When set, un-mould and serve with cream or with the Granit au Champagne (see page 36). The Edwardians would decorate the serving dish with a garland of flowers.

GRANIT AU CHAMPAGNE
CHAMPAGNE SORBET

Although I have not come across the word before, I am sure that 'granit' is another form of 'granita', which is a kind of sorbet. Champagne was often used in sorbets in the time of Edward VII, and pink champagne gives an especially attractive colour. Manually operated ice cream freezers allowed people to enjoy a range of ices, although they were hard work for the kitchen staff.

PREPARATION TIME: 10 MINUTES PLUS TIME FOR FREEZING

COOKING TIME: 5 MINUTES

SERVES: 6

150 ml (¼ pint) water

2 tablespoons lemon juice

75 g (3 oz) caster sugar

750 ml (1¼ pints) champagne (choose a variety that is not too dry)

Put the water, lemon juice and sugar into a saucepan. Stir over a low heat until the sugar has dissolved, then boil steadily for 3 minutes. Cool, then add the champagne and pour into an ice cream maker. Turn this until lightly frozen. Serve with the jellied Gâteau Punch (see page 35).

Variations

If you are making this sorbet without a modern ice cream maker, pour the mixture into a container and freeze lightly, then whisk with a fork until aerated and the surface is ridged. Return to the freezer but always serve lightly frozen.

Any sparkling wine could be used instead of champagne.

Gradins de Pâtisseries
Assorted Pastries

This course consisted of elegant trays of delicious pastries of the kind that are included in the banquet for the 1911 Coronation (see page 98–101).

CANAPÉS D'ANCHOIS À LA PROVENÇALE
ANCHOVY CANAPÉS À LA PROVENÇALE

These canapés consisted of crushed, freshly cooked anchovies mixed with various ingredients to make a savoury paste, not unlike the better-known tapenade. Canned anchovy fillets could be used (see Variations, below).

PREPARATION TIME: 15 MINUTES

COOKING TIME: 8–10 MINUTES

SERVES: 4

4 fresh anchovies

1 tablespoon extra virgin olive oil

1 tablespoon black olives, stoned

1 garlic clove

½ teaspoon chopped thyme

little French mustard

few drops of Worcestershire sauce

small toasted or fried croûtes, to serve

To garnish

1 egg, hard-boiled

finely chopped parsley

Cut the heads from the anchovies, brush the small fish with a few drops of oil and cook under a preheated grill until tender. Remove the skin and bone. Pound all the ingredients until smooth using a pestle and mortar. Spoon on the croûtes.

Chop the yolk and white of the egg separately and sprinkle over the anchovy paste. Top with parsley.

Variations

Use canned anchovy fillets. Do not heat these, but chop and then pound them with the other ingredients. The oil from the can should be used instead of olive oil.

For a luxury garnish chopped truffles would have been used.

PETITS SOUFFLÉS GLACÉS PRINCESSE

PRINCESS ICED PUDDING

A princess iced pudding, one of the favourites of this era, consists of a combination of aniseed and vanilla ice creams. For this banquet the iced mixtures were served in individual soufflé dishes. There are a variety of aniseed liqueurs, such as *anis del mone* from Spain, *ouzo* from Greece and *la tintaine* from France.

Aniseed Ice Cream

PREPARATION TIME: 20 MINUTES PLUS TIME FOR FREEZING

COOKING TIME: 10 MINUTES

SERVES: 8

2 eggs
50 g (2 oz) caster sugar
150 ml (¼ pint) single cream
1 tablespoon aniseed liqueur
300 ml (½ pint) double cream, whipped
25 g (1 oz) icing sugar, sifted

Separate the eggs. Put the yolks with the caster sugar and single cream into the top of a double saucepan or into a basin. Place over hot, but not boiling, water and whisk until thickened slightly. Remove from the heat, add the aniseed liqueur. Cover so a skin does not form and cool.

When cold, fold in the whipped cream. Whip the egg whites until very stiff. Whisk in the icing sugar and fold into the cream mixture. Put into an ice cream maker or a tray in the freezer and freeze lightly.

To assemble the dessert, spread the lightly frozen aniseed ice cream around the sides of individual soufflé dishes and fill the centres with the vanilla ice cream. Add more layers of lightly frozen ice cream until you have the effect of a soufflé that has risen above the rim of the soufflé dishes.

In Edwardian times each soufflé would be decorated with miniature bouquets of sugared flowers or crystallized fruits.

Serve the soufflés with *gaufrettes* (wafers).

Vanilla Ice Cream

Follow the directions for Aniseed Ice Cream (see left) but omit the aniseed liqueur and flavour the custard with ½–1 teaspoon vanilla extract (see above) or the seeds from 1 vanilla pod. Proceed as left.

Flavourings

In modern times we have become much more critical about the form of flavourings used. Even amateur cooks prefer to use a vanilla pod or the excellent vanilla extract rather than vanilla essence. I have suggested vanilla extract in some recipes, even where it would not have been available at the period when the dish was made. This is to ensure the best flavour. Vanilla pods have been used by first class chefs for a very long time, but they are now readily available in supermarkets for everyone to buy.

GEORGE V

REIGNED 1910-1936

WHEN PRINCE GEORGE WAS BORN ON 3 JULY 1865 AT MARLBOROUGH HOUSE, HIS GRANDMOTHER, QUEEN VICTORIA, WAS DELIGHTED THAT THE PRINCE AND PRINCESS OF WALES HAD A SECOND SON, BUT SHE DEMURRED AT THE PARENTS' CHOICE OF NAMES. SHE BELIEVED THAT HER DESCENDANTS SHOULD SELECT NAMES ONLY AFTER CONSULTING HER. SHE WAS EMPHATIC THAT SHE WANTED THE NAME ALBERT TO BE GIVEN TO EVERY BOY IN THE FAMILY IN MEMORY OF HER LATE HUSBAND.

Early Years

1865-1892

THE FIRST SON OF THE PRINCE AND PRINCESS, WHO HAD BEEN BORN IN 1864, WAS CALLED ALBERT VICTOR, BUT THE PRINCE OF WALES WAS ADAMANT THAT HE AND HIS WIFE WOULD CHOOSE THE NAMES THEY GAVE TO THEIR SECOND SON, AND IN SPITE OF HIS MOTHER'S DISLIKE OF TWO OF THEM, THE BABY WAS CHRISTENED GEORGE FREDERICK ERNEST ALBERT. THE PRINCE AND PRINCESS OF WALES WERE YOUNG PARENTS — THE PRINCE WAS ONLY 23 YEARS OLD AND THE PRINCESS WAS NOT YET 21 WHEN THEIR SECOND SON WAS BORN. THE WALES FAMILY WAS COMPLETED BY THE BIRTHS OF PRINCESSES LOUISE, MAUD AND VICTORIA. THE LAST CHILD, A BOY, DIED WITHIN A FEW HOURS OF HIS BIRTH.

Because there was less than two years between Albert Victor (known in the family as Eddy) and George, they tended to follow similar routines. The formal education of the two young princes was entrusted to the Rev. John Dalton, who stayed with the family for 14 years. George was much healthier than his older brother, and as he was the second son and not destined to be a future Prince of Wales and king it was decided that he should serve in the Navy. In 1877, when he was just 12 years old, it was planned that the boy should join the training ship *Britannia* as a naval cadet. Originally, there was no thought that Eddy should accompany him, but the Reverend Dalton pointed out to the parents and to Queen Victoria that Eddy depended so much on George that he would be at a loss without him. Dalton's point of view won the day, and the two boys joined *Britannia* together and their tutor went with them. The *Britannia* was based at Spithead; it was shore-based but run like a ship at sea. Prince George kept an account of his time on *Britannia* in which he described it 'as a pretty tough place'. The Princes were not given many special privileges, but they were allowed a private cabin.

When it was time to leave *Britannia* there was much discussion about the next stage in the two boys' development. Should they both go to sea together or should they be separated? In the end they both joined HMS *Bacchante* as midshipmen. During the next few years they voyaged to many countries, including the West Indies, South America, South Africa, Australia and Japan. The officers on board this ship were chosen with great care, and once again the Rev. Dalton accompanied them to supervise the boys and continue their education. Eventually he wrote a book, *The Cruise of H.M.S. Bacchante, 1879–1881*.

Prince George kept a diary of his travels, a habit he continued all his life. Someone who served aboard the ship wrote of the Prince: 'I never remembered Prince George losing his temper, unselfish, kindly, good-tempered, he was an ideal shipmate.'

Queen Victoria was not impressed by her grandsons' academic ability, particularly the fact they spoke little French or German. After leaving the ship, therefore, they spent six months in Switzerland to improve their languages, but it made little impression on them.

After returning from Switzerland Prince George was posted to HMS *Canada*, but this time his brother and his tutor did not join him, and he greatly missed them. The prince went on to serve on several ships, gaining naval experience and rising in rank. He kept his love of the sea throughout his life, and his service life gave him an appreciation of order and punctuality. In 1892 he was on leave at Sandringham when he developed typhoid fever – the disease that killed his grandfather Prince Albert and from which his father had suffered – but after a long convalescence he recovered. During this time a terrible thing happened to the royal family: in January 1892, when he had been celebrating his engagement to Princess May (Mary of Teck) and his 28th birthday, Prince Albert Victor died suddenly. He developed influenza, then inflammation of the lungs and died a few days later. Prince George was now the heir to the Prince of Wales and a future king.

Prince George was still weak after his own serious illness and genuinely desolate at the death of his brother. He felt ill equipped for his new position and realized that he would have to relinquish his much enjoyed career in the Navy, although he was allowed to command the cruiser *Melampus* for a short time. Queen Victoria conferred on him the title of Duke of York, and he went to Germany to represent the Queen at a golden wedding celebration. He stayed on for a time to try to master the German language without great success.

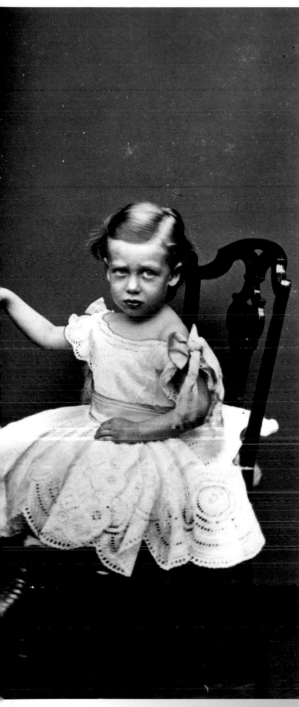

ABOVE: Prince George as a young child, *circa* 1867.

Marriage and After
1893

GEORGE'S FAMILY DECIDED THAT IT WAS TIME HE ACQUIRED A WIFE. THE PRINCE AND PRINCESS OF WALES AND THEIR FAMILY AND THE TECK FAMILY SPENT HOLIDAYS ON THE FRENCH RIVIERA. PRINCESS VICTORIA MARY (KNOWN AS MAY WITHIN THE FAMILY) HAD BEEN TAKEN ABROAD TO GET OVER THE SAD EVENT OF PRINCE ALBERT'S DEATH TO WHOM SHE HAD BEEN ENGAGED. MARY AND GEORGE GRADUALLY BECAME FRIENDS AND THEN FELL IN LOVE – AND FROM EVERY ACCOUNT THIS SEEMED GENUINE, AND NOT A MATTER OF ROYAL CONVENIENCE. THE COUPLE BECAME ENGAGED IN MAY 1893 AND WERE MARRIED IN JULY OF THAT YEAR.

The honeymoon was spent at York Cottage, which was a short walk from Sandringham. This was to be one of their homes for 33 years. In London they lived at York House, St James's Palace. The Yorks lived quietly and did not entertain as frequently as the Prince and Princess of Wales chose to do.

In June 1894 an heir was born. Knowing his grandmother's desire to name her descendants he wrote to her: 'Long before our dear child was born, both May and I settled that if it was a boy we should call him Edward after darling Eddy. This is the dearest wish of our hearts, dearest Grandmother, for Edward is indeed a sacred name to us.' The Queen was not impressed and replied: 'I think you write as if Edward was the real name of dear Eddy, while it was Albert Victor.' The baby prince was christened Edward Albert Christian George Andrew Patrick David; the family called him David.

ABOVE: Prince George with his wife Princess Mary of Teck on their honeymoon, *circa* 1893.

The second son, Albert Frederick Arthur George, was born in December 1895; he would later become George VI. Four more children followed: Princess Mary (who became the Princess Royal and Countess of Harewood), Prince Henry (later the Duke of Gloucester), Prince George (later the Duke of Kent) and the last born, Prince John, who died in January 1919 after years of illness.

In 1901, when Queen Victoria died and his father became Edward VII, the Duke and Duchess of York were preparing to visit Australia, where they would represent Queen Victoria and open the first parliament of the Commonwealth. Although King Edward and Queen Alexandra wanted their son to remain in Britain, it was decided that the tour should take place. The Duke and Duchess of York made a great success of their visits to Australia and Canada, and when they returned to England in November 1901 they received many congratulations. The Duke was created Prince of Wales a few days later.

The new Prince and Princess of Wales kept their home at York Cottage, Sandringham, refusing to move to a larger home. They made some use of Frogmore House near Windsor and moved from their quarters at St James's Palace to Marlborough House.

King Edward VII and his son were great companions at various personal and

ABOVE: Prince of Wales with four of his six young children in 1902. He went on to become King George V after his father, King Edward VII, died in 1910.

state occasions, and although Queen Alexandra appeared less devoted to her daughter-in-law she appreciated her care of her beloved son and her help with the problem of her 'beastly ears' (her deafness).

The Prince and Princess of Wales were conscientious parents but neither showed the kind of outward affection to their children that George had received from his father and mother. The couple carried out many engagements on behalf of the King, including a tour of India in 1905. Over the years the Prince, generally accompanied by his wife, visited various countries, and he became knowledgeable about the politics of the day. He was an outspoken man, and his sometimes brusque comments did not

please everyone. On 6 May 1910 Prince George wrote in his diary: 'At 11.45 p.m. beloved Papa passed peacefully away and I have lost my best friend and the best of fathers. I never had a word with him in my life.' The King had been carrying out his many royal social engagements to the end of his life. On the day of his death he insisted on dressing. The Prince of Wales told him that his horse Witch of Air had won the 4.15 race at Kempton Park, to which his father replied: 'Yes I have heard of it. I am very glad.' Those were the King's last words.

Queen Mary
1867-1953

ON HER CHRISTENING, THE BABY MARY (MAY) WAS GIVEN AN UNBELIEVABLY LONG LIST OF NAMES: VICTORIA MARY AUGUSTA LOUISA OLGA PAULINE CLAUDINE AGNES. SHE WAS BORN AT KENSINGTON PALACE, ON 26 MAY 1867. HER FATHER WAS PRINCE FRANCIS (LATER THE DUKE OF TECK), AND HER MOTHER WAS PRINCESS MARY ADELAIDE, A GRANDDAUGHTER OF GEORGE III. SHE SPENT HER EARLY YEARS IN ENGLAND AND, AS A GODDAUGHTER OF QUEEN VICTORIA, WAS VERY MUCH PART OF ENGLISH LIFE. ALTHOUGH THE TECK FAMILY WAS COMPARATIVELY POOR BY ROYAL STANDARDS GENEROUS FRIENDS HELPED THEM.

Between 1883 and 1885 the Teck family lived in Italy, and Princess May, who was already fluent in English, French and German, learned Italian, too, She also studied art and music, an interest that lasted throughout her life.

The Teck family returned to England in the spring of 1885 and made their home at White Lodge, Richmond. Although the Princess was never considered beautiful, she was described as pretty and she had great intelligence and dignity. Before her marriage, she had written in a letter to George: 'I am very sorry I am still so shy with you ... there is nothing I would not tell you, except I love you more than anybody in the world, and this I cannot tell you myself so I write it to relieve my feelings.' Prince George replied immediately: 'Thank God we both understand each other, and I think it really unnecessary for me to tell you how deep my love, for you, my darling is.'

The wedding took place in the Chapel Royal, St James's Palace, and Princess May had a superb trousseau, paid for by her aunt and uncle, the Grand Duke and Duchess of Mecklenburg-Strelitz. Sadly, the new Duchess of York's sisters-in-law were not over-friendly, mistaking her shyness for arrogance, but Queen Victoria was more far-seeing. 'Every time I see you,' she told May, 'I love and respect you – more and more and I am truly thankful that George has such a partner.'

During their life together Princess May was worried by her husband's outspoken manner, but her strongest expression of disapproval was only that it was 'not very nice'. The couple were not fond of foreign travel, but they greatly enjoyed their tour of India in 1905 and 1906, when they had become Prince and Princess of Wales. As King and Queen they went to India again in 1911–12 for the magnificent Durbar, when George was crowned Emperor of India. It is often said that Queen Mary's mode of dress never changed, but this was to please her husband, for she never forgot he was her sovereign, as well as her husband.

Later, during the First World War King George visited the front line, and in 1917 the Queen insisted on accompanying him, for she was concerned with the welfare of servicemen and with nursing. One of her favourite occupations was collecting any items that had any connection with the dynasty into which she had married, and she also created a wonderful doll's house.

Queen Mary had a quiet sense of humour and was friendly when she overcame her shyness. She nursed her husband devotedly during his illnesses, taking over more public appearances during his last illness. In her widowhood she made her home at Marlborough House, London, although during the Second World War she lived in Badminton, the home of her niece, the Duchess of Beaufort. She visited bombed towns and centres for the services. In 1945 she returned to London.

ABOVE: **Mary of Teck, who was born in Kensington Palace, London, and married Prince George in 1893.**

Queen Mary disapproved, without reservation, of divorce, and while George V was alive she insisted that divorced persons should not be allowed into the royal presence. She died on 24 March 1953, just before the Coronation of her beloved granddaughter, Elizabeth.

Events of 1910

ABOVE: Florence Nightingale (1820–1910) dies during this year after becoming the first woman to receive the Order of Merit for her tireless efforts during the Crimean War.

January

Trade figures for the British Empire reveal a rapidly expanding market of almost £350 million, of which Britain accounts for half.

In Paris floods threaten the Louvre, and thousands of people are forced to leave their homes.

In India five provinces are banned from holding 'seditious' meetings.

The police rescue Herbert Asquith, the Prime Minister, when he is mobbed by suffragettes in London.

The general election in Britain results in Conservative-Unionists 273, Liberals 275, Irish Nationalists 82, Labour 40; Asquith stays in power, confident of Labour support.

February

The first 80 Labour Exchanges open in Britain.

Switzerland, Germany and Italy agree to build a railway through the St Gothard Pass in the Alps.

In Glasgow the destroyer *Parramatta*, the first ship of the Australian Navy, is launched

March

D.W. Griffiths's first movie, *In Old California*, is made in Hollywood.

The Dalai Lama, forced out of Lhasa by the Chinese, is welcomed in India.

Mount Etna erupts, causing widespread destruction in Sicily.

April

The Prime Minister urges Edward VII to create new peers to swamp the anti-government majority in the House of Lords.

The House of Commons gives the first reading to a bill to abolish the veto of the House of Lords.

In federal elections in Australia the Liberal government loses to the Labour Party.

King Albert of the Belgians opens the World's Fair in Brussels.

May

The nation and world mourn the death of Edward VII.

In France Halley's Comet causes widespread concern and fears that it is responsible for bad weather.

A court in Westminster, London, rules that cabbies who ask for tips can be prosecuted.

June

Captain Robert Falcon Scott sets out to find the South Pole.

British explorers find pygmies in the mountains of Dutch New Guinea.

In Germany Count von Zeppelin's new airship flies with paying passengers.

The Spanish king, Alfonso XIII, proclaims freedom of belief.

July

The Union of South Africa becomes an independent dominion within the British Empire.

In Baltimore, Maryland, Duncan Black and Alonzo Decker found a tool company.

Speaking in Wales David Lloyd George states that reform of the House of Lords should take priority over women's suffrage.

The aviator Hubert Latham reaches a height of 15,240 m (50,000 ft) during trials at Rheims, France.

Dr Crippen is arrested aboard the SS *Montrose* off Quebec.

August

Soldiers and citizens throughout Britain pay tribute to the Lady of the Lamp, Florence Nightingale, who has died at the age of 90; among the tributes is one from Queen Alexandra, the Queen Mother.

The inventor Thomas Alva Edison demonstrates talking motion pictures at his laboratory in West Orange, New Jersey.

In London electric street lamps are replaced by 3,000 gas lamps, giving more light in fog.

In Brussels fire destroys much of the World's Fair, including works of art.

September

In London a doctor declares that if insanity continues to increase at the present rate the insane will outnumber the sane within 40 years.

In France the first pure sample of radium is isolated by Marie Curie.

In South Africa General Louis Botha, hero of the Boers fight against the British, loses his seat in the parliamentary elections but remains as Prime Minister as the Nationalist Party achieves a majority.

In Wales 10,000 miners go on strike in sympathy with dockers; cotton workers prepare to join them.

October

King Manuel II of Portugal is deposed in a revolution and flees to London; the new republican government orders the expulsion of all nuns and monks.

The White Star liner *Olympic*, the biggest vessel afloat, is launched in Britain.

In Paris a conference on cancer opens.

November

Russians flock to pay homage to the writer Leo Tolstoy, who has died in a simple hut, saying he wanted to die in peace.

Herbert Asquith, the Prime Minister, announces that the King will dissolve parliament and that the second election of the year will be over by Christmas.

Welsh miners accept a pay rise and call off their strike.

Suffragettes mob ministers in London, leaving one cabinet minister injured and confined to bed.

December

After some turbulent canvassing, the second election in Britain during 1910 also produces a dead heat: both Tories and Liberals have 272 seats.

Up to 350 men are feared dead following an explosion in a Lancashire pit, Britain's second worst mining disaster.

In New York Arturo Toscanini conducts the first performance of Puccini's opera *The Girl of the Golden West*.

ABOVE: Marie Curie, French physicist and winner of the 1903 Nobel Prize for Physics, isolates the first pure sample of radium.

Accession and After
1910

GEORGE V RODE ON HORSEBACK BEHIND HIS FATHER'S COFFIN ON 21 MAY 1910. THE FUNERAL CORTÈGE WAS FOLLOWED BY KAISER WILHELM, EIGHT KINGS, FIVE HEIRS APPARENT AND ABOUT 50 ROYAL PRINCES AND DUKES. SERVICEMEN FROM AROUND THE EMPIRE FORMED THE GUARD OF HONOUR. THE NEW KING ESCORTED HIS MOTHER, QUEEN ALEXANDRA, WHILE THE KAISER WALKED WITH QUEEN MARY. KAISER WILHELM GRUMBLED THAT HE HAD TO GIVE PRECEDENCE IN THE PROCESSION TO THE LATE KING'S FOX TERRIER.

LEFT: King George V and Queen Mary at Cowes, Isle of Wight with their eldest son.

In June 1910 King George's eldest son, known as David within the family, was created Prince of Wales at a ceremony at Caernarfon Castle, and in July of that year the King and Queen of the Belgians arrived for an official visit. King George and his wife moved to Buckingham Palace, and Queen Mary used the quiet period of court mourning to rearrange some of the apartments in her own style.

The Coronation of the new King took place on 22 June 1911, but before then King George and Queen Mary fulfilled several important duties. In February 1911 the King took part in the first State Opening of Parliament of his reign, describing it as 'the most terrible ordeal I have gone through'. In May 1911, just a few weeks before the Coronation, the King and Queen opened the Festival of Empire at the Crystal Palace in south London.

Although only nine years had elapsed between the Coronation of Edward VII and that of his son, the excitement in Britain was intense. Westminster Abbey was transformed by new, vivid blue carpets, and on the day itself there were

banks of red tulips, white lilies and blue delphiniums.

ABOVE: Detail of a patriotic postcard souvenir for the Coronation of George V in 1910.

It is reported that the King, Queen and Prince of Wales were nervous, but they acquitted themselves with great dignity throughout the seven hours of pageantry, and when the 16-year-old Prince of Wales paid homage to his father, the King embraced his son fondly.

In addition to the rows of peers and peeresses, the members of the royal families of Europe and dignitaries from many countries, there were princes from India in their colourful garments and

jewelled turbans, underlining the fact that the royal couple were also the Emperor and Empress of India.

George V was unique in having two coronations. On 11 November 1911 he sailed for India with the Queen and his advisers. The Great Durbar – the spectacular ceremony of coronation in India – was held on 12 December, and the royal party returned to Britain in February 1912.

Events of 1911

ABOVE: HMS *King George V*, Britain's latest and greatest battleship is launched during this year. It was armed with 10 14-inch guns and protected against aerial attack by very thick armour plating and a battery of anti-aircraft guns.

January

A house in Sidney Street, London burns to the ground together with two of the three 'anarchists' (who had already killed six policemen) trapped inside after a gun battle with 1,000 troops and armed police.

In Paris the Academie of Sciences debates the admission of women, but admits Henri Becquerel rather than Marie Curie, who is also a candidate.

In the UK the airship *Beta* transmits the first wireless message from the air.

February

James Ramsay MacDonald becomes chairman of the Labour Party in succession to James Keir Hardie.

Edward Mylius is sentenced to one year's imprisonment for libel in accusing George V of bigamy.

The Canadian parliament votes to remain within the British Empire.

Rolls-Royce commissions the 'Spirit of Ecstasy' statuette for their cars.

March

The British government proposes limiting the working week for shop-workers to 60 hours (excluding meal breaks).

Anna Rogstadt takes her seat as Norway's first woman member of parliament.

President Taft sends 30,000 soldiers to the Mexican frontier in case of revolution.

April

Despite reforms promised by President Porfirio Diaz of Mexico, rebellion breaks out, with US troops fighting on behalf of the rebels.

Women are refused the vote by the legislature of Massachusetts, while in Portugal the constitutional court establishes female suffrage.

Old Etonians, including the Duke of Marlborough, support the use of the birch for wrong-doers, saying it has more effect than writing lines.

In the FA Cup Final, Bradford City beats Newcastle United by 1–0.

French-Algerian forces combine with troops from Senegal to help the Sultan of Morocco in an uprising by tribesmen.

May

In Mexico, after almost 45 years in power, Porfirio Díaz is succeeded by the rebel leader Francisco Madero.

The Chancellor, David Lloyd George, unveils plans for a National Insurance scheme for British workers.

Sir W. S. Gilbert drowns in his swimming pool while trying to rescue a schoolgirl who was in difficulties.

The White Star liner SS *Titanic* is launched, becoming, with her sister ship *Olympic*, the largest vessel afloat.

June

Electric trolley buses come into service in Leeds and Bradford.

More than 40,000 supporters of votes for women march through London, ending with a meeting at the Albert Hall presided over by Emmeline Pankhurst.

July

Germany dispatches a gunboat, *Panther*, to the Moroccan port of Agadir amid concern in France and London about Gemany's motives.

Legislation gives shop-workers in Britain a half day off each week.

A heat wave in the USA causes 652 deaths within a week.

August

Leonardo da Vinci's *Mona Lisa* is stolen from the Louvre and is not recovered until December 1913.

The Parliament Bill curbs the powers of the House of Lords.

In Britain the dockers strike spreads to a nationwide strike of stevedores, railwaymen and other transport workers; 50,000 troops are called in to deal with the situation.

London is described as the second most unhealthy city in the world.

The House of Commons votes to pay members of parliament £400 a year.

September

In Paris the poet Guillaume Apollinaire is arrested, and later released, for the theft of the *Mona Lisa*.

In Kiev Russia's hard-line Prime Minister, Peter Stolypin, is assassinated in front of the tsar.

Thomas Burgess, a Yorkshireman, takes over 22 hours to swim from Dover to Cap Gris Nez.

In Belfast Sir Edward Carson rejects any possibility of Home Rule for Ireland.

Italy declares war on Turkey.

October

Winston Churchill is named as the new First Lord of the Admiralty.

The first Model-T Ford to be produced outside the USA rolls off the production line in Manchester.

The HMS *King George V*, the Royal Navy's biggest ship, is launched at Southampton.

November

More than 200 women suffragettes and a handful of men are arrested after riots in Whitehall, London.

A. J. Balfour resigns as leader of the Conservative Party and is replaced by Andrew Bonar Law.

Some 20,000 women (domestic workers and employers) fill the Albert Hall, London, to protest against plans to make householders pay National Insurance contributions for servants, saying this will lead to unemployment and cuts in servants' wages.

Joseph Pulitzer, the journalist and publisher who died in October, leaves an endowment for journalism prizes.

December

The Norwegian explorer Roald Amundsen reaches the South Pole ahead of the Briton, Captain Scott, who arrives in January 1912.

Marie Curie becomes a Nobel laureate for the second time, winning the chemistry prize for her discovery of radium and polonium.

At Nanking Sun Yat-sen is elected president of China by a provisional assembly.

ABOVE: King George V and Queen Mary at the Coronation Durbar in Delhi.

1911

THE CORONATION BANQUET

This menu shows distinct changes from the banquet held in 1902 (see page 28). George V and Queen Mary enjoyed simpler meals than Edward VII and Queen Alexandra, and they also enjoyed British ingredients. Turtle Soup had become a feature of grand banquets, and lamb was taking the place of mutton.

BUCKINGHAM PALACE BANQUET

◇

Tortue Claire

◇

Filets de Sole Britannia

◇

Canetons à l'Impérial

◇

Selles d'Agneau Princière

◇

Cailles à la Royale Flanquées d'Ortolans

◇

Asperges d'Argenteuil, Sauce Chantilly

◇

Pêches à la George V
Pâtisserie vVariée

◇

Cassolettes à l'Aurore

◇

Mousses de Fraises Reine Mary
Bonbonnières de Friandises
Gaufrettes

20 Juin, 1911

Their Majesties
KING GEORGE V & QUEEN MARY

TORTUE CLAIRE

TURTLE SOUP

Achieving a clear turtle soup was impossible for domestic cooks, for the large turtles were available only to palaces and large, well-to-do households. As I have never made turtle soup, I include information about the freshly prepared consommé by giving an excerpt from the instructions in *Larousse Gastronomique*. 'The carapace and plastron of the animal are cut into pieces of equal size, blanched for a few minutes in boiling water, cleaned of the outer shields that cover them, put into a big stew pot with richly flavoured consommé, savoury vegetables, turtle herbs (basil, marjoram, savory and thyme) and cooked like an ordinary broth for 6–7 hours.' The pieces of turtle would then be chopped and the liquid clarified to give a clear soup.

Variation

To enhance the flavour of canned turtle soup heat with a little dry sherry.

FILETS DE SOLE BRITANNIA

FILLETS OF SOLE BRITANNIA

The title of this dish is somewhat ambiguous, so I have included a classic recipe for cooking one of the world's finest white fish. This dish is generally called Filets de Sole Bercy.

PREPARATION TIME: 20 MINUTES

COOKING TIME: 35 MINUTES

SERVES: 4

4 large or 8 small sole fillets, skinned
bouquet garni
40 g (1½ oz) butter
2 shallots, finely chopped
2 teaspoons chopped parsley
300 ml (½ pint) dry white wine
150 ml (¼ pint) fish stock (see method)
25 g (1oz) flour
salt and pepper
lemon slices, to garnish

To make the fish stock, put the skin, bones and heads of the fish into a pan with water to cover and a bouquet garni. Simmer for 20 minutes then strain.

Fold the sole fillets in half, place them in an ovenproof dish greased with about 15 g (½ oz) of the butter. Add the shallots, parsley, half the wine, all the stock and a little salt and pepper. Cover the dish and cook in a preheated oven, 190°C (375°F), Gas Mark 5, for 20 minutes.

Lift the fish on to a heated dish and keep it warm. Strain the liquid from the dish. Heat the remaining butter in a saucepan, add the flour and stir over the heat for 2–3 minutes. Gradually incorporate the rest of the wine, plus the liquid from the dish. Bring to the boil, lower the heat and simmer for 10 minutes; season as required.

Coat the fish with the sauce, garnish and serve.

Variation

The sauce could be enriched by adding an extra knob of butter just before serving.

CANETONS À L'IMPERIAL

DUCKLING À L'IMPERIAL

For most of the 20th century all poultry was available with giblets, and these ducklings are cooked with an interesting stuffing based on the duck livers. The young birds are cooked twice: first by roasting and then by casseroling.

In the palace kitchens there would have been a choice of fats, and the fat used for the first stages of cooking the young ducklings could be goose fat. The truffles could be omitted.

PREPARATION TIME: 35 MINUTES

COOKING TIME: 1 ½ HOURS PLUS TIME TO MAKE THE GIBLET STOCK

SERVES: 4–6

2 ducklings with giblets (approximate weight 2.5 kg (5 lb)
600 ml (1 pint) duckling giblet stock (see method)
Stuffing
duckling livers, finely chopped
3 teaspoons finely grated orange rind
1 large onion, finely chopped
1 garlic clove, crushed
50 g (2 oz) truffle, thinly sliced (optional)
2 tablespoons chopped parsley
2 tablespoons soft breadcrumbs
2 tablespoons green olives, stoned and chopped
2 eggs
½ teaspoon chopped sage or ¼ teaspoon dried sage
salt and pepper
Roasting the ducklings
50 g (2 oz) butter or fat (see introduction)
Casseroling the ducklings
50 g (2 oz) flour
6 tablespoons brandy
12 very small onions or shallots
To garnish
orange slices
watercress
green olives

Put the giblets, except the livers, into water to cover. Simmer in a covered saucepan for 1 hour to produce 600 ml (1 pint) stock. Strain carefully.

Mix together all the stuffing ingredients and insert into the bodies of the two birds. Heat the butter or fat; brush over the ducklings. Place these on a trivet in a roasting tin and cook in a preheated oven, 200°C (400°F), Gas Mark 6, for 30 minutes. Lift the ducklings out of the oven and reduce the heat to 180°C (350°F), Gas Mark 4. Spoon the fat out of the roasting tin and add 2 tablespoons of this to a saucepan. Stir in the flour and continue stirring until there is a golden-brown roux. Gradually add the giblet stock, bring to the boil and cook until thickened, add the brandy and small onions or shallots, and season to taste with salt and pepper.

Put the ducklings back into the roasting tin without the trivet or into a large casserole. Carefully spoon the sauce and onions or shallots around, but not over, the birds. Cover the tin or casserole and cook for 1 hour.

Lift the ducklings on to a serving dish and garnish. Strain the sauce into a sauceboat. Serve with Orange Salad (see below).

Variation

In modern times the fat for cooking the ducklings would be omitted; early recipes of all kinds use a great deal of fat to cook meat and poultry.

ORANGE SALAD

In the early 20th century the classic orange salad was made by cutting away the peel and pith from sweet oranges, slicing the fruit, removing all the pips then flavouring the orange slices with Curaçao, rum, brandy or kirsch. A more elaborate version of this is known as Salade Marguerite, and this is an excellent accompaniment to duckling.

PREPARATION TIME: 20 MINUTES

SERVES: 4–6

1 endive, shredded

1 small lettuce, shredded

1 bunch white or black grapes

2 large oranges

1 small grapefruit

2–3 tablespoons blanched flaked almonds

Vinaigrette Dressing (see page 34)

Put the endive and lettuce into a salad bowl. Skin and deseed the grapes. Cut away the peel and pith from the oranges and grapefruit and cut out the segments of fruit. Discard all skin and pips.

Arrange the fruit on the lettuce and endive and top with the almonds. Add the vinaigrette dressing just before serving.

SELLES D'AGNEAU PRINCIÈRE

ROAST SADDLE OF LAMB

At the time of the Coronation much of the lamb would be young and milk-fed. In this dish the saddle (a double loin joint) is roasted. The term *princière* **means that truffles are included in the garnish, in addition to artichoke hearts and asparagus tartlets.**

For a smaller household a single loin joint or leg or shoulder of lamb would be more appropriate.

PREPARATION TIME: 1 HOUR (TO INCLUDE VARIOUS GARNISHES)

COOKING TIME: SEE METHOD

SERVES: DEPENDS ON SIZE OF JOINT

Weigh the meat and allow 18 minutes per 450 g (1 lb) and 18 minutes over. If the lamb is older, allow 20 minutes per 450 g (1 lb) and 20 minutes over. For pink (rare) meat allow just 15 minutes per 450 g (1 lb) and 15 minutes over. Put the meat into a preheated oven, 200–220°C (400–425°F), Gas Mark 6–7. If you are roasting a large joint, lower the heat to 190°C (375°F), Gas Mark 5, after 1 hour. Serve the meat with the following accompaniments (see right and page 56).

Artichoke Hearts and Truffles

Put fresh globe artichokes into boiling salted water and cook for about 20 minutes or until tender. The timing depends on the size of the artichoke. To check if cooked, pull away a leaf: the base should be very tender.

Cool, then strip away the leaves, remove the centre chokes and leave just the base, known as the heart.

Scrub the truffles, cut them into thin slices and heat for about 5 minutes in a generous amount of butter. Season with salt and pepper and spoon on to the artichoke hearts.

To give additional flavour and colour the artichoke hearts can first be topped with hot, well-seasoned, fresh tomato purée before adding the sliced truffles and any remaining butter.

Madeira Sauce

Madeira wines were extremely popular at the beginning of the 20th century, both for drinking and in cooking.

PREPARATION TIME: 30 MINUTES

COOKING TIME: 25 MINUTES

SERVES: 4–6

50 g (2 oz) butter or well-clarified dripping

1 medium onion, finely chopped

3 large mushrooms, sliced

2 medium tomatoes, chopped

25 g (1 oz) plain flour

300 ml (½ pint) brown stock

150 ml (¼ pint) Madeira wine

salt and pepper

Heat the butter or dripping in a saucepan, add the onion and cook for 3 minutes. Put in the mushrooms and tomatoes and cook for a further 5 minutes. Stir in the flour and cook gently for 2 minutes. Add the stock. Bring to the boil, season well with salt and pepper and cover the pan. Simmer for 10 minutes then rub through a sieve. Return to a clean saucepan, add the Madeira and heat thoroughly.

Asparagus Tartlets

Make small tartlet cases (see page 63) and cook fairly thin asparagus (see page 34). When the asparagus is tender cut off the tips for garnish. Sieve the tender stalks and mix with a little well-seasoned whipped cream.

Fill the tartlet cases with the asparagus purée and top with the asparagus tips. Serve the tartlets immediately after filling so that the pastry remains crisp.

Pommes de Terre à la Dauphinoise

This is an excellent way of cooking old floury potatoes. The dish should not be confused with Pommes de Terre Dauphine, in which creamed potatoes, enriched with a generous amount of butter and egg yolks, are mixed with choux pastry then formed into balls and fried.

In this dish wafer-thin slices of potato are baked in milk and egg, flavoured with cheese, nutmeg and garlic.

PREPARATION TIME: 25 MINUTES

COOKING TIME: 1 HOUR

SERVES: 4

50 g (2 oz) butter
1 garlic clove, halved
450 g (1 lb) potatoes, weight when peeled, cut into wafer-thin slices
300 ml (½ pint) milk
1 egg, whisked
pinch of grated nutmeg
100 g (3½ oz) Gruyère cheese, grated
salt and pepper

Spread about a quarter of the butter around the inside of a 1.2 litre (2 pint) ovenproof dish then rub the garlic over this.

Put the sliced potatoes into a basin. Heat the milk to boiling, remove from the heat and add the egg, salt and pepper, nutmeg and half the

cheese. Mix well with the potatoes then spoon into the prepared dish.

Top with the remaining cheese and small knobs of the remaining butter. Bake in a preheated oven, 190°C (375°F), Gas Mark 5, for 1 hour. Cut into portions to serve.

CAILLES À LA ROYALE FLANQUÉES D'ORTOLANS

ROAST QUAIL AND ORTOLANS

The inclusion of quail and ortolan in several of the Coronation banquet menus suggests that the royal family enjoys eating game birds. Each Coronation was held at a time when grouse, partridge, pheasant and the like were out of season, so these birds would be good alternatives.

A la royale is a custard-type garnish, usually served on clear soups, but it can be added to other foods, too. Larousse Gastronomique has many suggestions for cooking ortolan, including à la royale. I have used this simple, but luxurious, forcemeat in both the quails and the ortolans. Some more economical alternatives are suggested right.

PREPARATION TIME: 35 MINUTES

COOKING TIME: 15–21 MINUTES

SERVES: 4

8 quails, boned
8 ortolans, boned
115 g (4 oz) butter, melted
225 g (8 oz) foie gras
115 g (4 oz) truffle(s), very thinly sliced
salt and pepper
To garnish
Port Wine Sauce (see right)
shredded truffles, uncooked or heated in butter

Lay the boned birds on a board, skin side down. Brush the flesh with a little of the butter and season lightly with salt and pepper. Spread with the foie gras and add the truffle slices.

Form into neat shapes, enclosing all the forcemeat, and tie securely. Put the quails into a roasting tin; brush with some of the butter. Place in a preheated oven, 220°C (425°F), Gas Mark 7, and roast for 9–14 minutes, depending on size. Add the ortolans, brush with the last of the butter and continue roasting all the birds for 6–7 minutes. Remove the string.

Ortolans were usually served in individual dishes or pastry cases, but for this recipe, place one quail in the centre of an individual dish and put an ortolan on either side. Top with a little sauce and the garnish.

Variations

The birds could be cooked on a spit over a high heat.

Use Chicken Liver Pâte (see below) instead of foie gras and finely shredded mushrooms instead of truffles.

Chicken Liver Pâte

Heat 50 g (2 oz) butter with 2 teaspoons extra virgin olive oil in a frying pan. Add 1 small, finely chopped onion and cook gently for 3 minutes. Put in 1–2 crushed garlic cloves and continue cooking for another 2 minutes. Add 225 g (8 oz) chopped chicken livers. Fry gently for 5 minutes. Season well, then remove all ingredients from the pan. Add 1–2 tablespoons brandy or dry sherry or single cream to the pan and stir well to absorb the meat juices. Add to the liver and other ingredients then sieve or liquidize until smooth.

If storing, spoon into a dish and cover with a layer of melted butter.

The same weight of turkey, duck or goose liver could be used. Slice or dice the larger livers and cook until just tender.

ASPERGES D'ARGENTEUIL, SAUCE CHANTILLY

ASPARAGUS WITH CHANTILLY SAUCE

Asparagus from the Argenteuil region of France was considered to be some of the finest in the world, and it would be chosen for a royal banquet. The delicious light sauce is equally good with hot or cold asparagus. If you are serving the asparagus hot, start the preparations for the sauce in plenty of time so that the asparagus is served immediately it is cooked. If you are serving the asparagus and sauce cold, make the hollandaise sauce, whisk as it cools and then add the cream.

PREPARATION TIME: 20 MINUTES

COOKING TIME: 20 MINUTES

SERVES: 4

1 large bundle of asparagus
Hollandaise Sauce (see page 35)
150ml (¼ pint) double cream, whipped
salt and pepper

Cook the asparagus (see page 34) and make the hollandaise sauce.

To serve hot, gradually fold the whipped cream into the warm sauce in the same careful way the butter was added. Season to taste.

To serve cold, gently fold the cream into the cold sauce, then add salt and pepper to taste.

Variation

Another form of chantilly sauce is made by seasoning whipped cream and flavouring it with a generous amount of lemon juice.

Port Wine Sauce

Follow the instructions for Madeira Sauce on page 55 but substitute port wine for Madeira wine. A few drops of truffle oil could be added.

PÊCHES À LA GEORGE V

PEACHES À LA GEORGE V

This dessert incorporates a number of different flavours, and the zabaglione complements them better if it is made with champagne rather than the usual Marsala. After a fairly generous main course the dessert would serve eight.

PREPARATION TIME: 25 MINUTES

COOKING TIME: 6–8 MINUTES

SERVES: 4–8

4 large, ripe peaches

225 g (8 oz) alpine (wild) strawberries

25 g (1 oz) caster sugar

2 tablespoons kirsch

2 tablespoons maraschino liqueur

Zabaglione

4 egg yolks

4 tablespoons caster sugar

4–6 tablespoons champagne or Marsala

Lower the peaches into boiling water, leave for 30 seconds then put them in cold water. Pull away the skins. Halve and stone the fruit and arrange on a flat dish or individual plates. Top with the small strawberries, making neat pyramids of these. Mix the sugar with the kirsch and maraschino and spoon over the fruit.

Make the zabaglione. Put the egg yolks and sugar into a basin over a pan of hot, but not boiling, water. Whisk briskly until thick and creamy. Add the champagne or Marsala in small amounts and slowly, making sure each additional amount of liquid is absorbed before adding any more. Spoon the warm zabaglione over the fruit and serve.

Variation

In some classic recipes for this dessert, the zabaglione is served cold. Sliced ordinary strawberries could replace alpine strawberries.

Pâtisseries Variée

See the recipes on page 98–101.

CASSOLETTES À L'AURORE

RAMEKINS À L'AURORE

The word *cassolette* describes small dishes that can be heated in the oven or under the grill. They were used to present individual portions of hors d'oeuvre, savouries or hot desserts.

   ***Aurore* describes a tomato-flavoured velouté sauce. At the time of this banquet, easy-to-use, concentrated tomato purée would not be available; sieved fresh tomato pulp would be used instead.**

PREPARATION TIME: 25 MINUTES

COOKING TIME: 15 MINUTES PLUS TIME TO MAKE THE STOCK, COOK THE
   EGGS AND HADDOCK

SERVES: 4

Sauce

25 g (1 oz) butter

25 g (1 oz) plain flour

300 ml (½ pint) white (veal or chicken) stock

2 tablespoons very thick tomato purée

1 tablespoon dry sherry (optional)

salt and pepper

Filling

4 eggs, hard-boiled

**225 g (8 oz) cooked smoked haddock, weight when boned
   and skinned**

Topping

50 g (2 oz) Gruyère cheese, grated

Heat the butter in a saucepan, mix in the flour and stir over a low heat for 2–3 minutes. Add the stock, bring to the boil and cook until thickened and smooth. Add the tomato purée, sherry and season with salt and pepper.

Cut the shelled eggs in slices. Flake the fish and put it into the dishes with the eggs and sauce to cover. Top with a thick layer of cheese and heat under a preheated grill until golden brown.

Serve with fingers of crisp toast.

Variations

Add diced cooked or canned anchovy fillets to the sauce and eggs in place of the haddock.

Omit the cheese topping and add fine buttered crumbs instead.

MOUSSES DE FRAISES REINE MARY

STRAWBERRY MOUSSE QUEEN MARY

These strawberry-flavoured desserts are simple to make. The mixture of fruit, sugar and cream can either be well chilled or lightly frozen. This is the type of mousse that would have been served at the time of the Coronation, and it does not contain gelatine or egg whites.

PREPARATION TIME: 20 MINUTES

SERVES: 6-8

450 g (1 lb) ripe strawberries
600 ml (1 pint) double cream
100 g (3½ oz) caster sugar, or to taste
small strawberries and/or crystallized rose petals, to decorate

Rub the strawberries through a non-metal sieve. Whip the cream until very stiff. Fold the purée into the cream and add the sugar. Spoon the mixture into individual dishes and chill well or lightly freeze. Do not serve when too firm. Decorate and serve with *gaufrettes* (wafers).

BONBONNIÈRES DE FRIANDISES

PETITS FOURS

A *bonbonnière* is a dish to hold bonbons (sweetmeats); *friandises* are titbits, so these would be dishes of petits fours, which might include various chocolates, marrons glacés, marzipan fruits, miniature macaroons (ratafias) and tiny brandy snaps (see page 94). There might also be Florentines. In this recipe all ingredients should be cut very small.

Florentines

PREPARATION TIME: 30 MINUTES

COOKING TIME: FROM 6 MINUTES (SEE METHOD)

MAKES: 18–40, DEPENDING ON SIZE

85 g (3 oz) unsalted butter
85 g (3 oz) caster sugar
115 g (4 oz) almonds, blanched and cut into thin slivers
50 g (2 oz) candied peel, very finely chopped
50 g (1 oz) glacé cherries, finely chopped
25 g (1 oz) sultanas, finely chopped
1 level tablespoon plain flour
1 tablespoon double cream
150 g (5 oz) plain chocolate, to coat

Melt the butter and sugar over a very low heat, add the nuts, peel, cherries and sultanas, cool then stir in the flour and cream.

Put small spoonfuls of the mixture on to greased baking sheets, allowing plenty of room for them to spread. Bake in a preheated oven, 180°C (350°F), Gas Mark 4, for 6–10 minutes, depending on the size. Check the baking carefully for these biscuits burn easily. When set enough to handle, remove from the baking sheets. You can gently pull the edges inwards to neaten the shape.

Allow the biscuits to get quite cold. Melt the chocolate over hot, but not boiling, water, coat the underside of each florentine and allow to set. They can be stored for several days in a tin away from other biscuits.

1911

THE STREET PARTY

When George V was crowned, snack-type meals, with the exception of sandwiches, were less well known than they are today, and a special festive meal would probably have included a 'meat tea'. Salad would be served with the cold meats, and salad cream would have been the accompaniment. Mayonnaise and vinaigrette dressing were not popular or even known by most ordinary people. Some adults loved pickled onions, which they ate with any cold meat, so a recipe is given.

Children were less fussy in those days and were happy to share the same food as their parents. They would enjoy cakes as well as a dessert.

CORONATION STREET PARTY MENU 1911
BOILED BACON
OX-TONGUE
MIXED SALAD WITH SALAD CREAM
PICKLED ONIONS
FRUIT SALAD WITH CUSTARD SAUCE
BAKEWELL TART
JAM AND LEMON CURD TARTS

BOILED BACON

Brief instructions are given on page 33 for boiling gammon. Most housewives would buy a cheaper bacon joint, such as collar or forehock, for a street party. In the early part of the century, bacon was fairly heavily salted and would need to be soaked.

PREPARATION TIME: 20 MINUTES PLUS OVERNIGHT SOAKING

COOKING TIME: SEE METHOD

SERVES: SEE METHOD

bacon collar or forehock

few onions

few carrots

bunch of parsley

pepper or 1–2 teaspoons peppercorns

crisp breadcrumbs, to coat (see method)

Put the bacon in cold water to cover. Leave overnight then pour away the water. Put the bacon, with the whole vegetables, parsley and fresh water to cover, into a saucepan, add a good shake of pepper or the peppercorns.

Bring the water to simmering point, then cover the pan and time the cooking. For collar or forehock bacon joints, allow 40–45 minutes per 450 g (1 lb). For gammon see page 33. Allow the bacon joint to cool in the liquid so that it keeps moist.

When cold, remove the bacon from the stock, drain and cut away the rind. Press the crisp breadcrumbs against the fat.

For a joint weighing about 2 kg (4 lb) before cooking, you need about 50 g (2 oz) crisp crumbs. This would serve 8–10 people.

OX-TONGUE

Ox-tongue was a favourite cold meat at the time and an ideal choice for a large number of people. Butchers sold them ready salted.

PREPARATION TIME: 35 MINUTES PLUS OVERNIGHT SOAKING

COOKING TIME: SEE METHOD

SERVES: ABOUT 12, DEPENDING ON SIZE

1 salted ox-tongue

2 onions

2 bay leaves or 1 dried bay leaf

2–3 pieces of lemon rind

1 teaspoon peppercorns

1 teaspoon powder gelatine or 2 gelatine leaves

Wash the ox-tongue well, then soak in cold water overnight. Drain the tongue and discard the water. Put the ox-tongue with all the ingredients, except the gelatine, into a large saucepan and cover with water. Bring to boiling point then lower the heat, cover the pan and simmer steadily. Allow 40 minutes per 450 g (1 lb).

Remove the tongue from the liquid and allow to cool. Strain the stock then boil in an open pan until just under 300 ml (scant ½ pint) remains. Allow to cool. Meanwhile, skin the tongue and remove all the small bones.

Roll the meat and fit it tightly (to give a good shape) into a round saucepan or cake tin. Soften the gelatine in the cold stock for 3 minutes then heat until dissolved. Strain over the tongue. Place a plate over the top of the meat and add a light weight to press the meat. Leave until cold and the jellied stock has set, then slice thinly and serve.

MIXED SALAD

Throughout most of the 20th century in Britain, a mixed salad would consist of lettuce leaves, sometimes shredded, sometimes left whole, with sliced tomatoes, cucumber, hard-boiled egg and radishes. Sliced, cooked beetroot was generally served separately.

Salad Cream

This was the favourite accompaniment to a salad. It could be purchased from a grocer's shop, but many people preferred to make their own.

PREPARATION TIME: 15 MINUTES

COOKING TIME: 18 MINUTES

SERVES: 4–6

450 ml (¾ pint) milk

1 onion, sliced

1 small carrot, sliced

½ celery stick, chopped

25 g (1 oz) butter

25 g (1 oz) plain flour

1–2 egg yolks, whisked

1–2 tablespoons white wine or white malt vinegar

salt and pepper

Bring the milk with the vegetables just to boiling point, then put on one side until cold. Strain the milk.

Heat the butter in a saucepan, stir in the flour then gradually add the milk. Whisk or stir until thickened then remove from the heat. Blend the egg or eggs with half the vinegar and add to the sauce. Return to the heat and whisk over a very low heat for 5 minutes, season to taste with salt and pepper and add more vinegar to give the desired taste. Whisk the sauce as it cools to prevent a skin forming, then serve or pour into a screw-topped jar. Store in a cool place but use within 2–3 days.

PICKLED ONIONS

For many people in the 1910s, cold meat was incomplete without pickled onions. Although they could be purchased in jars, many people preferred to prepare them at home, and they took a pride in producing jars of perfect onions.

PREPARATION TIME: 40 MINUTES PLUS BRINING (SEE METHOD)

MAKES: 2 MEDIUM JARS

about 750 g (1½ lb) small pickling (silverskin) onions
Wet brine
50 g (2 oz) kitchen salt or sea salt
600 ml (1 pint) water
Spiced vinegar
600 ml (1 pint) white malt or white wine vinegar
1 teaspoon mixed pickling spice, or to taste

The purpose of brining vegetables before pickling is to draw out the water content. Simply mix the salt and water together.

Always prepare the onions with a stainless steel knife to prevent the outsides darkening. Remove the skins. Put the onions into the wet brine and place a plate on top to make sure the onions are well covered. For a crisp result leave for 24 hours; for a softer texture leave for 36–48 hours.

Make the spiced vinegar. Vinegar for pickling must have 5 or 6 per cent acetic acid. Boil the vinegar and pickling spice for 5 minutes. Check the flavour and if it is inadequately flavoured boil for another 5 minutes. Cool and strain.

Drain the onions, rinse in plenty of cold water and drain again. Pack into cold, sterilized jars and cover with cold, sterilized vinegar. Seal the jars and cover tightly. Never put metal covers directly over preserves containing vinegar; put a thick piece of cardboard under the metal.

Variation

More pickling spice can be used, in which case check the boiling time carefully.

FRUIT SALAD

At the time of the Coronation most families in Britain would eat a relatively small amount of fruit, but adults and children would enjoy the opportunity to sample a mixture of fruits. Canned fruit was available and so were bottles of the more interesting fruits, such as sliced peaches.

Fruit from a can or jar generally formed the basis of a fruit salad and then seasonal fruits would be added. At the time of the Coronation there would be early strawberries, so they would be mixed with dessert apples, sliced bananas, stoned cherries and orange segments and the diced or sliced preserved fruit.

Custard Sauce

Although custard powder was readily available, many people made the traditional egg custard. Vanilla pods might be unavailable to many people, so they would use vanilla essence, the extract being unobtainable at the time (see page 37).

PREPARATION TIME: 10 MINUTES

COOKING TIME: 10–12 MINUTES

SERVES: 4–6

2 egg yolks
2 eggs
25–40 g (1–1½ oz) caster sugar
600 ml (1 pint) milk
1 vanilla pod

Beat the egg yolks and eggs with the sugar. Heat the milk with the vanilla pod. Add to the eggs and sugar then strain into the top of a double saucepan or basin over a saucepan of hot, but not boiling, water.

Whisk briskly until the custard thickens sufficiently to coat the back of a wooden spoon. Remove from the heat, take out the vanilla pod, cool slightly then pour into a serving jug. Cover to prevent a skin forming. Serve hot or cold.

BAKEWELL TART

This traditional recipe is sometimes called Bakewell Pudding. There are more luxurious recipes than the one described below, but this would be the version made by most people. In 1911 many people would grind blanched almonds at home; ready–prepared ground almonds would be used today.

PREPARATION TIME: 30 MINUTES

COOKING TIME: 40–45 MINUTES

SERVES: 6

Shortcrust pastry

175 g (6 oz) plain flour

pinch of salt

85 g (3 oz) fat (half lard and half butter or margarine)

water to bind

Filling

3 tablespoons raspberry jam

85 g (3 oz) butter or margarine

85 g (3 oz) caster sugar

1 egg, whisked

25 g (1 oz) plain flour

85 g (3 oz) ground almonds

40 g (1½ oz) fine cake or soft breadcrumbs

2 tablespoons milk

To decorate

2 tablespoons icing sugar

Sift the flour and salt into a mixing bowl, rub in the fat until the mixture is like fine breadcrumbs. Add the water gradually to give a firm rolling consistency. Wrap and chill for a short time if possible, then roll out and line a 20–23 cm (8–9 inch) flan tin.

Spread the base of the pastry with the jam. Cream the butter or margarine with the sugar and the egg, then the remaining ingredients. Spread over the jam.

Bake in a preheated oven, 190°C (375°F), Gas Mark 5, for 40–45 minutes or until firm. Check after 30 minutes and lower the heat slightly if the filling is becoming too brown. Allow to cool and top with sifted icing sugar. Cut in slices to serve.

JAM TARTS

Choose several jams with different flavours so there is a variety of colours in the tarts.

PREPARATION TIME: 20 MINUTES

COOKING TIME: 12–15 MINUTES

MAKES: 15–18

Shortcrust Pastry (made with 175 g (6 oz), see left)

various jams

Make the pastry. Roll it out, cut into rounds with a pastry cutter and line patty tins. Put a small spoonful of jam into each pastry case; do not overfill because this causes the jam to boil out of the pastry during cooking.

Bake in a preheated oven, 200°C (400°F), Gas Mark 6, for 12–15 minutes. Add a little extra jam to each tart.

For special occasions, the filling can be topped with a small amount of whipped cream.

Lemon Curd Tarts

Line the patty tins with the pastry and prick the base with a fork. Lemon curd is spoiled by overheating, so it is better to bake the pastry cases blind (empty). Bake for 10–12 minutes at the oven temperature above or until firm in texture. Add the lemon curd to the cold tartlets.

The Broadcaster King

George V was the first monarch to broadcast to his people. At first he was disinclined to do this, but friends and advisers persuaded him to make his first broadcast in April 1924 when he opened the British Empire Exhibition at Wembley. Some of his other speeches were broadcast, and at Christmas 1932 he made his first Christmas broadcast over the radio.

Silver Jubilee of George V

1935

ALTHOUGH KING GEORGE V WAS TOUCHED BY THE WELCOME THAT GREETED HIS SILVER JUBILEE CELEBRATIONS ON 6 MAY 1935, HE DEPLORED THE FUSS AND EXPENSE, FOR HE ALWAYS LIVED IN A COMPARATIVELY MODEST MANNER WHILE UPHOLDING THE GRANDEUR OF STATE OCCASIONS.

Accompanied by Queen Mary, the King rode through brightly decorated streets to St Paul's Cathedral for the service. There were 4,406 people in the cathedral, including visiting royalty and ambassadors. The King wore the uniform of a field marshal, and Queen Mary was in white, with a necklace of pearls and brilliant stones. Three generations of the King's family were present – the Queen; his own children, including Edward, Prince of Wales, and Prince George; and his two young granddaughters, the Princesses Elizabeth and Margaret.

The cheering crowds were the largest that had been seen in London since Armistice Day, 1918. Broadcasting from Buckingham Palace that evening, the King said: 'I can only say to you my very, very, dear people, that the Queen and I thank you from the depths of our hearts for all the loyalty – and may I say so? – the love, with which this day and always you have surrounded us.'

The days that followed were filled with appearances on the Palace balcony, and a special ceremony at St James's Palace for representatives of the Empire, described 'as the most touching and homely triumph of ceremony and loyal homage ever held'.

No one was more surprised at the many expressions of affection during Jubilee summer than the King himself. 'I didn't realize they felt like this,' he said.

After the excitement of the Jubilee celebrations the King and Queen resumed their familiar routine of visiting Cowes in the Isle of Wight, Sandringham and Balmoral. In December the King delivered the Christmas broadcast with his usual skill, but it was apparent that his voice had grown weaker, and in the New Year he gradually became less and less well, until it was obvious that he was extremely ill. He died at 11.55 p.m. on 20 January 1936. Queen Mary had cared for her husband throughout his lifetime, and on his death she kissed the hand of her eldest son, Prince Edward, in homage. He had become the new King.

BELOW: The Royal procession to Buckingham Palace from the Thanksgiving Service at St. Paul's Cathedral on the Silver Jubilee of King George V.

Events

of

1935

ABOVE: Sir Malcolm
Campbell sitting in his new
Bluebird car at Brooklands
after setting the new land
speed record of over
484 kph (301 mph).

January

Commercial flights between London
and Australia are inaugurated by
Imperial Airways and Qantas.
The French and Italian governments
reach agreement over their problems
in Africa.
More than 90 per cent of the
population of the Saarland votes to
be reunited with Germany.

February

In Berlin Adolf Hitler opens the
world's largest motor show.
Italy sends troops to Ethiopia.
The USA signs a trade agreement
with Brazil.
In Turkey women are allowed to vote
in the general election.
Mary ('America's Sweetheart')
divorces Douglas Fairbanks.
RADAR (RAdio Detection And
Ranging) is demonstrated at
Daventry by Robert Watson-Watt.

March

The League of Nations returns the
Saar region to Germany.
The British government publicly
acknowledge the need for
rearmament.
Germany introduces conscription, in
direct contravention of the Treaty of
Versailles.
A speed limit of 48kph (30mph) is
imposed in built-up areas in Britain.
Persia is renamed Iran.

April

Italy, France and Britain protest
at German rearmament and agree

to act together.
'Cat's eyes' are first used on
Britain's roads.
Dust storms rage over Kansas,
Colorado, Oklahoma and Texas,
destroying wheat crops and forcing
people to flee.

May

Britain celebrates George V's Silver
Jubilee.
The Left Book Club, founded
by Victor Gollancz, publishes its
first title.
Stanley Baldwin announces the
expansion of the Royal Air Force.
T.E. Lawrence (Lawrence of Arabia)
dies in a motorcycle accident.
The American athlete Jesse Owens
breaks 5 world records within 45
minutes at Ann Arbor in Michigan.

June

The French liner SS Normandie
arrives in New York after crossing
the Atlantic in 4 days, 11 hours,
33 minutes.
Stanley Baldwin becomes Prime
Minister when Ramsay MacDonald
retires.
Alcoholics Anonymous is founded in
Akron, Ohio.
Driving tests introduced in Britain by
Transport Minister Leslie Hore-Belisha
and 'L' plates made compulsory.

July

The United States signs a trade pact
with the USSR.
Anti-Catholic riots break out in
Belfast, Northern Ireland.

Fred Perry becomes men's champion at Wimbledon; Helen Wills Moody is women's champion.

The Third International declares that communists throughout the world should support their governments in the fight against fascism.

Parking meters come into operation in Oklahoma, USA.

Allen Lane publishes the first Penguin paperbacks.

August

Burma, Aden, Kuwait and other dependencies are separated from India by the Government of India Act.

Vitamin E is isolated by US scientists.

President Roosevelt signs the Neutrality Act, which prohibits the shipping of arms to warring countries.

Queen Astrid of Belgium is killed when a car driven by her husband King Leopold III careers off a road near Lucerne and crashes into a tree.

September

The 'Nuremberg Laws' are passed in Germany, banning Jews from the professions and outlawing marriage with non-Jews.

The Swastika becomes Germany's official flag.

Florida's East Coast Railroad is destroyed in a hurricane, killing 400 people.

Sir Malcolm Campbell sets land-speed record of over 484 kph (301 mph) at Bonneville Salt Flats, Utah.

Senator Huey Long of Louisiana is assassinated by Dr Carl Weiss.

October

Italy invades Ethiopia, leading the League of Nations to impose sanctions against Italy.

Mao Zedong and about 6,000 survivors reach Yan'an (Yenan) after the 'Long March' of 9,600 km (6,000 miles).

George Gershwin's *Porgy and Bess* is premiered in New York.

November

The Commonwealth of the Philippines becomes largely self-governing.

In the British general election Baldwin's government has a majority of 245 seats.

Clement Attlee becomes leader of the British Labour party.

Japan invades Peking.

US balloonists Anderson and Stevens reach a heaight of 22,555 m (74,000 ft).

Non-belief in Nazism becomes grounds for divorce in Germany.

December

Chiang Kai-shek is elected president of the Guomindang executive.

The president of Czechoslovakia, Tomás Masaryk, resigns and is succeeded by Eduard Benes.

Sir James Chadwick receives the Nobel prize for physics.

The composer Alban Berg dies.

ABOVE: English tennis champion Fred Perry (1909–1995) leaping over the net to shake hands with his opponent after winning the Wimbledon men's single final.

1935

JUBILEE STREET PARTY

In the 1930s many parts of Britain were experiencing high levels of unemployment, but that did not prevent street parties being organized to celebrate the King's Silver Jubilee.

In the 25 years since the Coronation, tastes in food appear to have changed very little, and the menu below includes many of the dishes that would have been served at the parties throughout Britain. The economical buns, jelly and blancmange would be a treat for poor children, and the ingredients would have been within the price range of their parents. The savoury dishes and trifle would be made by better-off families.

THE MENU

CORNISH PASTIES

SALMON TURNOVERS

PORK PIE

RUSSIAN SALAD

POTATO SALAD

FRUIT TRIFLE

BANANA JELLY AND BLANCMANGE

CHELSEA BUNS

ICED SWISS BUNS

LEMONADE

CORNISH PASTIES

These traditional pasties are ideal for street parties. They would be made smaller than usual if younger children were among the guests.

PREPARATION TIME: 30 MINUTES

COOKING TIME: 35–40 MINUTES

MAKES: 8

Shortcrust pastry

375 g (12 oz) plain flour

175 g (6 oz) fat (half lard and half butter or margarine)

water to bind

pinch of salt

Filling

300 g (10 oz) tender steak, such as rump

2 medium potatoes, finely chopped

2 medium onions, finely chopped

2 teaspoons chopped parsley

2 teaspoons beef stock

salt and pepper

1 egg, beaten, to glaze

Make the pastry as described on page 63. Roll out and cut into 8 rounds with a large pastry cutter or cut around a small saucer.

Cut the meat into very small dice and mix with the other ingredients for the filling. Place small amounts in the centre of the pastry rounds. Moisten the edges of the pastry with water then bring them together to form the traditional pasty shape. Seal firmly.

Put on a baking sheet and brush with the egg. Bake in a preheated oven, 200°C (400°F), Gas Mark 6, for 20 minutes, then lower the heat to 180°C (350°F), Gas Mark 4 and continue cooking until golden and firm.

Salmon Turnovers

Fill the pastry (see Cornish Pasties, left) with 300 g (10 oz) finely diced uncooked salmon or well-drained canned salmon, diced potatoes and a little chopped onion together with 3–4 tablespoons peeled and diced cucumber and seasoning. Moisten the filling with 1–2 teaspoons lemon juice.

Instead of making an upright pasty shape, fold the moistened pastry over the filling to give the shape of a turnover and glaze. Bake as for the Cornish Pasties.

PORK PIE

In the 1930s home baking was fashionable, and ambitious cooks made excellent meat pies. The pastry used for this type of raised pie is known as hot water crust (see right).

PREPARATION TIME: 35 MINUTES

COOKING TIME: 2½ HOURS

SERVES: 6

Filling

675 g (1½ lb) lean pork from the leg, diced

225 g (8 oz) fat pork from the belly, diced

3 tablespoons veal or chicken stock

salt and pepper

Pastry

hot water crust made with 375 g (12 oz) flour (see right)

To glaze

1 egg, beaten

Jelly

1 teaspoon gelatine

150 ml (¼ pint) veal or chicken stock

Mix the two kinds of pork with the stock and season to taste.

Make the pastry as described and use while warm. Lightly grease an 18–20 cm (7–8 inch) cake tin, preferably one with a loose base, or a special raised pie springform tin. Roll out enough pastry to line the base and sides of the tin. Press it in the prepared tin. Fill with the pork.

Moisten the top edges of the pastry with a little water. Roll out the remaining pastry and cut out a shape for the lid of the pie. Arrange over the top of the pie and seal the edges.

Make a slit in the centre of the pastry lid. Use any pastry left over to make leaf shapes and press in position on the top of the pastry. Brush with the beaten egg.

Bake in a preheated oven, 160°C (325°F), Gas Mark 3, for 2½ hours. Slightly reduce the heat of the oven after 2 hours if the pastry is becoming too brown.

Allow the pie to cool. Soften the gelatine in the cold stock, then heat until the gelatine dissolves. Allow to cool and become the consistency of a thick syrup. Insert a small funnel into the slit in the pastry lid and pour the jelly through this. Chill for several hours to allow the jelly to set. Serve.

Hot Water Crust Pastry

This is the correct pastry for raised pies. The instructions above describe how to use the pastry in a tin, but expert pie-makers would mould (known as raising) the pastry to form a shape without a tin. Using milk (rather than water) gives a richer pastry.

PREPARATION TIME: 15 MINUTES

COOKING TIME: SEE RECIPE

SERVES: SEE RECIPE

150 ml (¼ pint) milk or water

115 g (good 4 oz) lard or cooking fat

375 g (12 oz) plain flour

¼ teaspoon salt

Put the milk or water and fat into a saucepan. Heat until the fat melts. Remove from the heat. Sift the flour and salt into the saucepan and stir briskly until well mixed.

Allow to cool sufficiently to handle, and then knead until smooth. Use while warm. This pastry cracks badly if allowed to become cold before it is used.

RUSSIAN SALAD

The mixture of diced cooked vegetables is both colourful and appetizing. The vegetables should retain a firm texture. In the 1930s many people would mix the ingredients together with a salad dressing, but mayonnaise is much better.

PREPARATION TIME: 30 MINUTES

COOKING TIME: 15–25 MINUTES

SERVES: 6–8

150 g (5 oz) young carrots, diced
150 g (5 oz) new potatoes, diced
50 g (2 oz) young turnip, diced
50 g (2 oz) young swede, diced
150 g (5 oz) green beans, sliced
50 g (2 oz) peas
salt and pepper
Salad Cream (see page 61) or Mayonnaise (see page 129)
chopped parsley, to garnish

Cook the vegetables separately or in one saucepan in boiling salted water, adjusting the cooking time for each type. Strain thoroughly and mix with the salad dressing or mayonnaise while still hot.

Cool and spoon into a serving dish then top with chopped parsley.

Variation

An authentic Russian Salad contains cooked meats or poultry, and up to 375 g (12 oz) diced cooked beef, ox-tongue, ham or chicken could be mixed with the vegetables. For this variation, top the salad with chopped hard-boiled egg as well as parsley.

POTATO SALAD

The best potato salad is made by adding the selected dressing to the hot potatoes. In 1936 Salad Cream (see page 61) would be chosen by many people, but the combination of oil, vinegar and Mayonnaise, as in the recipe below, gives the best flavour.

PREPARATION TIME: 20 MINUTES

COOKING TIME: ABOUT 20 MINUTES

SERVES: 6

450 g (1 lb) potatoes, preferably new
2 tablespoons extra virgin olive oil*
1 tablespoon white wine vinegar
2–3 tablespoons Mayonnaise (see page 129)
salt and pepper
1 tablespoon finely chopped parsley
2 tablespoons finely snipped chives

* This type of oil would be known only by people who had travelled abroad. It would have been omitted by most people. The majority of people would have been happy to use only salad cream .

Cook the potatoes in salted water until just tender; do not overcook. Strain and dice. Stir the oil, vinegar and mayonnaise together and mix with the hot potatoes, season well with salt and pepper. Allow to cool then add the herbs.

Variations

This is a basic salad, but other ingredients such as diced celery heart or diced dessert apple, a few chopped capers and additional herbs could be added.

Finely chopped spring onions could replace the chives.

Diced avocados might now be added to the salad; they are an excellent addition to the potatoes.

FRUIT TRIFLE

PREPARATION TIME: 25 MINUTES

COOKING TIME: 10–12 MINUTES

SERVES: 6–8

6–8 trifle sponge cakes

3–4 tablespoons raspberry jam

450 g (1 lb) canned fruit salad plus syrup from the can

1–2 tablespoons orange juice

600 ml (1 pint) Custard Sauce (see page 62)

To decorate

150 ml (¼ pint) double cream, whipped

few glacé cherries

small piece of angelica, cut into leaf shapes

few blanched almonds

Split the sponge cakes then sandwich the halves together with the jam. Put them into one serving dish or several individual containers. For a street party, use disposable containers. Drain the fruit salad and mix the syrup with the orange juice; moisten the sponge cakes with this liquid, making them soft but not too soggy.

Chop the pieces of canned fruit into small pieces and spoon over the sponges.

Prepare the custard and pour it, while still warm, over the other ingredients. Cover the container or dishes to prevent a skin forming and leave until the custard is cold. Decorate with the cream, cherries, angelica and almonds.

Variations

To make Sherry Trifle, use 150 ml (¼ pint) sweet sherry instead of that amount of fruit syrup.

Jellied Trifle

Make up a jelly with a jelly tablet but use the syrup from the can plus water to give the quantity of liquid advised on the jelly packet.

Add the fruit salad as the recipe above then pour the jelly over the trifle sponges while it is hot. Allow the jelly to set then add the custard. When the custard is cold decorate as before.

BANANA JELLY AND BLANCMANGE

Jelly and blancmange had become one of the acknowledged food partnerships by 1936. Jelly tablets were inexpensive and easy to prepare, and bananas were a favourite fruit. Blancmange powders, in various flavours, had superseded the more elaborate dessert recipe of the Victorian era, and it was quite usual to set the jelly and blancmange in fancy moulds, such as those shaped like rabbits.

PREPARATION TIME: 15 MINUTES

COOKING TIME: 10 MINUTES

SERVES: 4–6

Banana Jelly

1 orange or raspberry jelly tablet

just under 600 ml (1 pint) boiling water

2 bananas, sliced

Blancmange

1 packet strawberry or other flavoured blancmange powder

600 ml (1 pint) milk

25–50 g (1–2 oz) caster sugar

Break up the jelly tablet and put the squares into a basin. Pour over the boiling water and stir until all the jelly dissolves. Allow to become quite cold, then add the sliced bananas.

Rinse a jelly mould with cold water; shake out the surplus moisture then pour in the jelly and leave until set. Dip the mould into hot water for a few seconds and invert on to the serving dish.

Make the blancmange. Put the powder into a basin, stir in just under one-quarter of the cold milk to make a smooth mixture. Heat the rest of the milk with the sugar. Pour on to the blancmange powder, then return to the saucepan and stir over a low heat until the mixture thickens. Pour into a mould rinsed out with cold water. Leave until set then invert on to a serving dish.

CHELSEA BUNS

In 1936 fresh yeast was readily available and would have been used to make the dough. The recipe below is based on modern fast-acting yeast, which needs only one rising (proving) but see Variations below. The amount of yeast is generous to balance the richer ingredients. The unglazed buns freeze well.

PREPARATION TIME: 30 MINUTES PLUS ABOUT 45 MINUTES FOR THE DOUGH TO RISE

COOKING TIME: 15 MINUTES

MAKES: 9–12

Enriched yeast dough

375 g (12 oz) strong white flour

pinch of salt

1 tablespoon or 1 sachet fast-acting dried yeast

25–50 g (1–2 oz) caster sugar

50 g (2 oz) butter or margarine

about 150 ml (¼ pint) milk (see method)

1 egg, whisked

Filling

50 g (2 oz) butter or margarine

50 g (2 oz) soft light brown or caster sugar

100 g (3½ oz) mixed dried fruit

pinch of ground cinnamon

pinch of ground nutmeg

To glaze

2 tablespoons caster sugar

2 tablespoons boiling water

Sift the flour and salt into a mixing bowl. Add the yeast and sugar. Rub in the butter or margarine.

Warm the milk to blood heat, 43°C (110°F), add to the flour, then put in the egg. Mix thoroughly. For these particular buns the dough should have a soft rolling consistency, so add a little more liquid if necessary – do not have it too dry.

Turn the dough out on a board and knead by stretching the dough until smooth. Roll out to a large long oblong shape, 1.5 cm (½ inch) thick.

Mix the filling ingredients together; spread evenly over the dough. Roll

loosely (to allow space for the dough to rise) then cut into 9–12 portions.

Place with the cut sides uppermost in a lightly greased 23–25 cm (9–10 inch) square cake tin. Cover the top of the tin with clingfilm and leave in a warm place for the buns to rise until nearly double in size. This should take about 45 minutes.

Bake in a preheated oven, 220°C (425°F), Gas Mark 7, for 15 minutes or until firm and golden brown. Lift the buns out of the tin. Mix the sugar and boiling water together and brush over the hot buns. Place on a wire rack. Serve freshly made.

Variations

Use 15 g (½ oz) fresh yeast. Cream with a teaspoon of the sugar, add the warm liquid and a sprinkling of flour. Leave until the surface is covered with bubbles then add to the flour and other ingredients and continue as above. Allow the dough to rise, then knead again and roll out, add the filling and continue as the recipe above.

You can place the uncooked buns on a flat baking sheet rather than in a cake tin. Pack fairly closely so they keep a good shape.

ICED SWISS BUNS

The dough for these buns needs to be a little softer than it is for Chelsea Buns. The quantity is based on making rather small buns. The uncooked buns freeze well.

PREPARATION TIME: 15–20 MINUTES PLUS ABOUT 45 MINUTES FOR THE DOUGH
  TO RISE

COOKING TIME: 12–15 MINUTES

MAKES: 16–18 BUNS

Enriched Yeast Dough (see left)
1–2 tablespoons milk
Glacé Icing, made with 225 g (8 oz) icing sugar (see below)

Prepare the dough as for Chelsea buns, but make it a little softer. Knead until smooth, then divide into 16–18 portions. Roll these into finger shapes. Put on lightly greased baking sheets, allowing room for the buns to spread slightly in cooking. Leave to prove (rise) as for Chelsea buns. Bake in a preheated oven, 220°F (425°F), Gas Mark 7, for 12–15 minutes. Lift the hot buns on to a wire rack and leave to cool.

Make the glacé icing and spread a little on top of each bun. Leave until the icing has set. Serve when freshly made.

Glacé Icing

This is often called water icing, although lemon or orange juice can be used instead of water. Sifted cocoa, chocolate or instant coffee powder can be mixed with the icing sugar.

PREPARATION TIME: 5 MINUTES

MAKES: ENOUGH TO COAT THE TOP OF AN 18 CM (7 INCH) CAKE OR
  EQUIVALENT IN SMALL CAKES

225 g (8 oz) icing sugar, sifted
water to mix

Put the icing sugar into a basin then gradually beat in sufficient water to make a soft consistency that can be spread over a cake or biscuits.

When using glacé icing to decorate cakes or biscuits first tint the icing with a few drops of food colouring, if needed. Then, put the icing into a piping bag with a very small plain nozzle and pipe out the shapes required.

LEMONADE

This was the popular way of preparing home-made lemonade. The flavour is fairly intense, so each glass would be about one-third filled with lemonade and topped up with water.

PREPARATION TIME: 20 MINUTES

COOKING TIME: 5 MINUTES

SERVES: ABOUT 10

2 large lemons
900 ml (1½ pints) water
2 tablespoons sugar

Halve the lemons, squeeze out the juice and put on one side. Remove all the pips from the lemon halves. Put the lemon halves into a saucepan and add the water and sugar. Bring to the boil and simmer for 3–4 minutes. Cool, strain, then add the lemon juice.

Orangeade

Use 2 large oranges instead of lemons. For a drink with more flavour add 1 lemon to the oranges.

GEORGE VI
REIGNED 1936–1952

PRINCE ALBERT FREDERICK GEORGE (CALLED BERTIE BY THE FAMILY) WAS THE SECOND SON OF THE PRINCE AND PRINCESS OF WALES (LATER GEORGE V AND QUEEN MARY). HIS ELDER BROTHER, EDWARD (KNOWN AS DAVID), WAS LESS THAN TWO YEARS OLDER, SO THE BOYS WERE GOOD COMPANIONS AND SPENT MUCH TIME TOGETHER. EVEN WHEN THEY WERE YOUNG THEIR FATHER DECIDED THAT THEY WOULD FOLLOW HIM INTO THE NAVY. IN 1902 HE APPOINTED HENRY HANSELL AS THEIR TUTOR, BECAUSE AT THE TIME HE DID NOT APPROVE OF BOYS BEING SENT AWAY TO SCHOOL, ALTHOUGH HE CHANGED HIS MIND WITH HIS TWO YOUNGER SONS, HENRY AND GEORGE.

Early Years
1908-1936

MR HANSELL HAD TAUGHT IN PREPARATORY AND PUBLIC SCHOOLS, AND HE EXCELLED AT SPORTS. UNFORTUNATELY, HE WAS NOT A GIFTED TEACHER. THEIR MOTHER WAS HORRIFIED THAT THE BOYS HAD NOT LEARNED FRENCH OR GERMAN, AND THE PRINCE OF WALES ENGAGED A SPECIAL TUTOR TO COACH HIS OLDER SONS SO THAT THEY COULD GAIN ENTRY TO THE NAVAL COLLEGE AT OSBORNE IN 1909. AFTER OSBORNE, ALBERT (LATER TO BECOME KING GEORGE V) WENT ON TO THE ROYAL NAVAL COLLEGE, DARTMOUTH, WHERE HE STAYED UNTIL 1913.

On the outbreak of war in 1914, Prince Albert was serving as a midshipman on HMS Collingwood. The Prince of Wales, his elder brother, joined the Grenadier Guards, so the King and Queen shared the worries of countless parents who had sons in the forces. Although his naval career was interrupted by gastric illnesses, necessitating operations, at the Battle of Jutland in May 1916 Prince Albert was in a gun turret on his ship and was mentioned in dispatches.

After his years in the Navy, Prince Albert served with the Naval branch of the Royal Air Force, becoming a qualified pilot, although the King never flew and hated the thought of his sons flying. He was in Germany with the RAF when he met Princess Victoria, sister of the exiled Kaiser. The Prince wrote to his father telling him about the meeting: 'She asked after you and the family and hoped we would be friends again. I told her I did not think that would be possible for a great many years!'

The Prince, who was created Duke of York in 1920, had a speech impediment, which made him nervous about official occasions, especially when he was required to make a speech. Not long after his marriage he was fortunate enough to meet an Australian speech therapist, who gave him a great deal of help and the confidence that improved his delivery a great deal.

It was the suggestion of King George V that his second son, spent a year at Trinity College, Cambridge studying consitutional history. This was under the quiet influence of Queen Mary, who remembered the fact that her husband had become heir to the throne only because of his elder brother's death. She wanted to ensure that her second son had at least some preparation, in case such an event could occur again.

The Prince was extremely good at tennis and played in the mens' doubles at Wimbledon. He was a caring man who was genuinely interested in the welfare of people.

RIGHT: George VI playing as a young child.

LEFT: George VI as a young boy (far right) with his brothers and father, King George V.

Marriage and After

1923

THE DUKE FELL IN LOVE WITH LADY ELIZABETH BOWES-LYON, A DAUGHTER OF THE EARL AND COUNTESS OF STRATHMORE. AS A DEBUTANTE SHE HAD BEEN GREATLY ADMIRED, FOR SHE WAS NOT ONLY VERY PRETTY BUT WAS FULL OF VITALITY AND HAD GREAT CHARM. MANY YOUNG MEN FOUND HER IRRESISTIBLE. IN 1922 THE PRINCE PROPOSED AND WAS EVENTUALLY ACCEPTED. THEY WERE MARRIED ON 26 APRIL 1923.

The Duke and Duchess of York, who were not particularly wealthy, made their first home at White Lodge, Richmond Park, but this proved too large and expensive, so they moved to town, to 145 Piccadilly. They lived happily and modestly there, not entertaining lavishly. In 1931 the King offered them the Royal Lodge in Windsor Great Park, and they and their young daughters, Elizabeth and Margaret, lived there happily.

The Duke became president of the Industrial Welfare Society, which gave him a good knowledge of industry and working conditions, and he toured the country to visit industrial areas. This led him to found the Duke of York's annual camps for boys, and newspaper photographs showed the Duke happily singing along with the boys.

The Duke and Duchess sailed on HMS *Renown* in January 1927 for a tour of New Zealand and Australia. They left their baby daughter in the care of the King and Queen. The Duke had to deliver many speeches on this tour, which he did with great success, and everyone was enchanted with the Duchess. The King was so impressed with their achievements that he ordered the Duke's brothers to greet the couple at Portsmouth on 27 June, and he and Queen Mary met them at Victoria Station.

As the years went by, it was obvious that the Yorks enjoyed an almost idyllic family life. The King increasingly grew to appreciate the virtues of his second son, who carried out many important engagements. In contrast, the behaviour of the Prince of Wales was a cause for concern. The British press had agreed not to publish details about his close friendship with Mrs Wallis Simpson, even though the overseas newspapers were full of stories about their relationship.

When George V died on 20 January 1936 Edward accepted the Crown and ruled for most of 1936. The world, including the Duke and Duchess of York, were horrified when he abdicated on 12 December 1936. Albert then became king, as George VI.

RIGHT: Duke of York and Lady Elizabeth Bowes-Lyon at Lady Elizabeth's London residence on their engagement day.

LEFT: The wedding of the Duke of York and Lady Elizabeth Bowes-Lyon.

Queen Elizabeth, the Queen Mother
1900–

ON 4 AUGUST 1900, ELIZABETH ANGELA MARGUERITE BOWES-LYON, WHO WOULD BECOME A DUCHESS AND LATER QUEEN CONSORT TO GEORGE VI, WAS BORN. SHE WAS THE NINTH CHILD OF CLAUDE BOWES-LYON, 14TH EARL OF STRATHMORE, AND HER FAMILY'S LINEAGE COULD BE TRACED BACK TO ROBERT BRUCE, KING OF SCOTLAND IN THE 14TH CENTURY. AS A CHILD SHE LIVED IN THE FAMILY HOMES OF ST PAUL'S WALDEN BURY IN HERTFORDSHIRE AND GLAMIS CASTLE IN SCOTLAND, AND ALTHOUGH ELIZABETH WAS BORN IN ENGLAND, SHE ALWAYS CONSIDERED HERSELF SCOTTISH.

Most of Elizabeth's siblings were considerably older than she was, but two years after her birth her brother David was born. Her parents were conscientious and affectionate, and Lady Elizabeth's childhood was exceptionally happy. Her nurse was called Allah, and when Elizabeth became Duchess of York years later and gave birth to her first daughter, who was to become Elizabeth II, Allah was in charge of the nursery.

Although Lady Elizabeth had a governess she was also sent for a short time to a day school in London, a quite exceptional thing for girls of the time. Her mother spent time teaching her children how to read and also teaching them French, history and other subjects.

The happy, serene life changed with the outbreak of war, which happened on Elizabeth's 14th birthday, 4 August 1914. The family was quickly affected by the war.

LEFT: Elizabeth with her daughters arriving at Glamis Castle, Scotland, to present Colours to the 4th and 5th Black Watch Regiments.

Four of Elizabeth's elder brothers joined their regiments, and one was killed in action. Glamis Castle, the family's Scottish home, became a convalescent home for wounded personnel; although still only a teenager Elizabeth played an important part in cheering the patients and helping her mother run the household.

When the war ended, Elizabeth had matured into a beautiful young lady, and one of the most attractive debutantes of the season. When she was 19 years old she met Prince Albert, who was then aged 24, and the prince told a family friend that he had fallen in love at first sight. The young people had a mutual friend in Lady Airlie, and she arranged that the prince, now Duke of York, should visit Elizabeth in Scotland. The duke was enchanted by the relaxed atmosphere and wrote to Queen Mary: 'It is delightful here and Elizabeth is very kind to me. The more I see her, the more I like her'.

Things did not go quite as the Duke would have wished. He proposed twice and was refused because Elizabeth was not sure if she wanted to embrace the many problems of marrying into the royal family. Queen Mary arranged that she and her son should be invited to Glamis Castle, and when they were there she realized that Lady Elizabeth would make a perfect wife for her son. The third time he proposed, she said 'yes', and on 26 April 1923 the couple were married at Westminster Abbey. The country rejoiced, and King George V and Queen Mary were delighted with their new daughter-in-law.

Like all the members of the royal family Elizabeth appreciated the problems that lay ahead when George V died, but she was even more saddened and concerned when the abdication of Edward VIII meant that her husband became king. She knew that his health was not robust and feared that the strain and responsibilities that he would carry would affect him seriously.

Throughout the war years they shared in the danger of living in London – Buckingham Palace itself was damaged – and visited the badly bombed areas. After the war the Queen realized that the strain of the past years had tired both the King and herself. She wrote to Queen Mary to say she 'was quite exhausted seeing so much sadness, sorrow, heroism and magnificent spirit. The destruction is so awful and the people are so wonderful they deserve a better world.'

The people of Britain had grown to admire their King and Queen and regarded them with great affection. Sadly, during the next years the King's health deteriorated, and he died in the early hours of 6 February 1952.

Events of 1936

ABOVE: Jesse Owens (1913–1980) at the start of the 200 metres at the 1936 Berlin Olympics which he won in 20.7 seconds, an Olympic record. He also won three other gold medals, in the 100 metres, 4 x 100 metres relay and long jump.

January

In London it is reported that the RAF will expand at the rate of a squadron a week.

Rudyard Kipling, writer and poet, dies.

In Washington the National Democratic Committee endorses F. D. Roosevelt's candidacy in the 1936 presidential election.

February

Britain wins its first gold medal, for ice hockey, in the Winter Olympics at Garmisch-Partenkirchen, Germany.

Adolf Hitler launches the 'people's car', the Volkswagen.

The Swiss government refuses entry to members of the Nazi party.

Charlie Chaplin's film *Modern Times* opens in the USA.

March

In defiance of the treaties of Versailles and Locarno, the Nazis enter the Rhineland.

The Vickers Spitfire I goes on show for the first time at Eastleigh aerodrome near Southampton.

In Rome, Mussolini states that he will nationalize the main industries.

April

The government of Austria re-introduces military service in violation of the peace treaties.

In Egypt, the 16-year-old Crown Prince Farouk is proclaimed king on the unexpected death of his father, King Faud.

In London, the government puts 3d in the pound on income tax.

Arsenal beats Sheffield United in the FA Cup by 1 goal to 0.

May

The SS *Queen Mary*, Britain's 80,733-ton super liner, leaves Southampton on her maiden voyage.

The Emperor Haile Selassie and his family flee when Italy annexes Ethiopia.

The aviator Amy Johnson arrives back in London after a return flight to Cape Town in a record 12 days, 15 hours.

The BBC appoints its first two women announcers, and Leslie Mitchell becomes the first TV announcer.

June

The SS *Queen Mary* arrives in New York to a tumultuous welcome.

Gatwick airport opens.

Both Britain and France abandon the sanctions imposed against Italy because of the action against Ethiopia.

Haile Selassie addresses the League of Nations in Geneva.

July

Fascist rebels under General Franco rise against the Republican government of Spain, which appeals for foreign help in the civil war.

Edward VIII visits France to unveil the memorial to Canadians who fell at Vimy Ridge during the First World War.

In Britain, the GPO's Speaking Clock service begins, and 248,828 calls are made in the first week.

Britain wins the Davis Cup tennis trophy for the fourth successive year.

August

It is rumoured that an attempt will be made on the life of Edward VIII as he presents new colours to six Guards battalions; George McMahon, a journalist, who has a revolver, is seized by a policeman before he can fire it.

Fred Perry wins the Men's Singles at Wimbledon for the third year running.

Adolf Hitler opens the Olympics in Berlin; Jesse Owens from the USA wins four gold medals.

Nearly 7,000 people queue at Olympia in London to see the first ever talking pictures on BBC Television, which are transmitted from Alexandra Palace, some 16 km (10 miles) away.

September

General Franco's rebels are poised to attack Madrid.

In Britain, 130,000,000 stamps bearing King Edward VIII's head are sold in the first five days.

In India, a massive landslide destroys seven Himalayan villages.

In London, a study shows that the average family needs £6.00 a week to keep it above the 'poverty line'.

October

In Britain, 200 unemployed men begin their long march from Jarrow to London, bearing a petition with 11,572 signatures to force attention on the 65 per cent unemployment in the town.

Spanish government forces prevent Franco's advance on Madrid.

A train ferry service between Dover in England and Dunkirk in France allows people to board a train in London and disembark in Paris.

A typhoon strikes the Philippines, killing many people.

November

King Edward VIII opens the first parliament of his reign and spends two days reviewing the fleet.

In the East End of London 100,000 people clash with the 7,000 black-shirted fascist supporters of Sir Oswald Mosley.

Industrialist, Lord Nuffield, gives £2,000,000 to Oxford University for a medical research school.

Crystal Palace, built in 1851 for the Great Exhibition in Hyde Park, and later moved to Sydenham, catches fire.

Roosevelt elected for a second term as President of the USA.

December

King Edward VIII abdicates to marry Wallis Simpson.

In Spain 5,000 Germans join Franco's forces.

Anthony Eden, the British foreign secretary, urges Germany not to support Franco, in Spain.

Sir Henry Dale from Britain and Otto Loewi from Austria share the Nobel prize for medicine.

Salvador Dali, the Surrealist painter, lectures in London wearing a diving suit; it is eventually found that his helmet has stuck, almost suffocating him.

ABOVE: The *Daily Express* newspaper headline carrying the story of the abdication of King Edward VIII, and the coming Coronation of his brother, George, in his place.

Accession and After

1936

ON 20 JANUARY 1936 THE PRINCE OF WALES BECAME KING AS EDWARD VIII. HE HAD ALWAYS BEEN POPULAR, AND AT THE OUTSET OF HIS REIGN THERE WAS NO REASON TO SUPPOSE HE WOULD NOT BE CROWNED. THE WHOLE OF BRITAIN – INDEED, THE WHOLE WORLD – WAS SHOCKED WHEN HE RENOUNCED THE THRONE ON 10 DECEMBER 1936. HIS BROTHER, PRINCE ALBERT, THE DUKE OF YORK, BECAME KING AS GEORGE VI, AND ON 12 DECEMBER 1936 A NEWSPAPER HEADLINE READ: 'SHY BERTIE SUCCEEDS AS GEORGE VI.' IT WENT ON TO SAY THAT 'THE NEW KING ADDRESSED THE ACCESSION COUNCIL IN A LOW SLIGHTLY HALTING NERVOUS VOICE'.

Prince Albert decided he would take the title George VI, to follow his father, George V. He approached his new role with trepidation, for he appreciated that he had much to learn. He had never had access to state papers or talked with politicians and had always been in the shadow of his elder brother, who, as Prince of Wales, had impressed people in Britain and overseas with his easy charm. On the other hand, over the years, Prince Albert had become closer to his father and had learned from his example. The new King was a man who was willing to take advice and who had the support of his loving wife.

The Coronation of the new King took place within a relatively short time, on 12 May 1937. There do not appear to have been any specific preparations for his Coronation, but this is not surprising, for the initial planning would have been done during the short reign of Edward VIII.

When he came to the throne George VI had a multitude of problems. He had to meet and become acquainted with his ministers, the government and officials, but fortunately, he was a man who was prepared to listen and learn and was an instinctive judge of character. There were also family problems concerning the Duke of Windsor, the name taken by Edward VIII on his abdication.

The Coronation was a great success, and the royal family settled into their new residences at Buckingham Palace and Windsor Castle, which were so different from their cosy family home. The King and Queen paid Coronation visits to various parts of Britain, and in July 1937, while they were visiting Belfast, a bomb exploded close to the couple. Throughout 1937 anxiety about a possible war in Europe intensified, and in November of that year the government decided to erect air raid shelters in major towns and cities.

In July 1938 the royal couple received a rapturous reception when they visited France. In the land of fashion, Queen Elizabeth's clothes received great approval.

In June 1939 they went to New York to visit the World Fair at the personal invitation of President Roosevelt, after a very successful tour of Canada.

RIGHT: A Cardiff factory worker moulding papier-mâché shields for the Coronation celebrations.

Events of 1937

ABOVE: Margot Fonteyn (1919–1991) in the title role of *Giselle* with Alexis Rassine.

January

London protests to Franco about the shelling of a British steamer, *Blackhill*, off northern Spain.

The 18-year-old ballerina, Margot Fonteyn, triumphs in London in the title role in *Giselle*.

Horse-drawn traffic is banned from the West End of London.

Both the UK and USA ban volunteers from fighting in Spain, but idealists from all over the world make their way there.

February

The Chancellor, Neville Chamberlain, reveals the new high figures for British defence. In Paris similar steps are taken to match Germany's arms budget.

In Britain petrol rises by 1/2d to 1s 7d a gallon.

In the USA, the manmade fabric nylon is patented.

March

A survey shows there are 800 millionaires in Britain.

The Australians win the fifth test against England at cricket and retain the Ashes.

In Paris, the British conductor Sir Thomas Beecham is presented with the Légion d'honneur.

April

London County Council proposes a 'green belt' around London to create space for recreation and to prevent urban sprawl.

Guernica, the cultural and spiritual home of the Basques, is destroyed by the German air force, sent to help Franco by Adolf Hitler.

The *Ark Royal*, Britain's largest aircraft carrier, is launched at Birkenhead.

Leon Trotsky, the inspiration behind international communism, now living in Mexico, calls for the overthrow of Stalin.

May

The German giant airship *Hindenburg* explodes over Lakehurst, New Jersey.

Neville Chamberlain becomes Prime Minister when Stanley Baldwin retires.

Margaret Mitchell wins the Pulitzer Prize for her novel *Gone with the Wind*.

The BBC's first television outside broadcast shows the Coronation procession of George VI.

June

The former Edward VIII, now known as the Duke of Windsor, marries Mrs Wallis Simpson near Tours, France.

Jean Harlow, the American film actress, dies from a kidney disease in a Los Angeles hospital at the age of 26.

Catholic youths clash with Nazis in Germany.

In Jerusalem, a Royal Commission looks into the possibility of a divided Palestine.

In Moscow, eight generals are shot as spies.

In Spain, Bilbao falls to Franco's rebels. The Nazis close all Catholic schools in Bavaria.

July

American aviator Amelia Earhart disappears on the last half of a round-the-world flight from California.

The American composer George Gershwin dies from a brain tumour at the age of 36.

The express train Coronation Scot reaches Edinburgh in a record 6 hours from London.

Japan attacks China from the puppet empire of Manchukuo.

The 999 telephone emergency service comes into use in Britain.

August

The British runner Sydney Wooderson sets a new world record for the mile handicap race.

Britain offers to mediate in the Sino-Japanese war as Britons and other foreign residents leave Shanghai due to bombing from Manchukuo.

Three German journalists are expelled from London while the Nazis expel *The Times* correspondent from Berlin.

September

Yorkshire defeats Hampshire to clinch the County Cricket Championship.

Japan refuses to apologize for wounding the British ambassador in China in the bombing offensive.

General Chiang Kai-shek and Mao Zedong, the communist leader, join forces to combat the Japanese.

The British speed ace, Sir Malcolm Campbell, sets a new world water speed record of 141 kph (129 mph).

October

The Duke and Duchess of Windsor visit Berlin and meet Adolf Hitler.

President Roosevelt condemns Japanese aggression in China.

King George VI opens the first parliament of his reign.

The first London Motor Show opens at Earl's Court, London.

November

In London it is announced that the BBC will begin broadcasting in Spanish, Portuguese and Arabic.

MPs vote in favour of preparing air-raid shelters in most of Britain's cities and towns.

In Germany parents are told their children will be taken from them if they do not teach them Nazi ideology.

The House of Commons pays tribute to Ramsay MacDonald, who died at sea, *en route* to America.

December

The Japanese reach the outskirts of Shanghai and occupy Nanking.

Joseph Kennedy is made the new American Ambassador to Britain.

From Geneva it was stated that Italy has left the League of Nations.

Viscount Cecil of Chelwood, President of the League of Nations Council, is awarded the Nobel peace prize.

In Dublin, the new constitution comes into force. The republic is called Eire.

In China, the Japanese army occupies Nanking.

Italy leaves the League of Nations.

Brazil bans political parties.

ABOVE: The German-built *Hindenburg* catches fire in the stern while trying to land at the Lakehurst Naval Air Station, New Jersey. The ship was engulfed in flames and crashed in less than a minute. Thirty-six people were killed in the disaster.

1937

THE CORONATION OF GEORGE VI

The Coronation of George VI was judged to have been carried out faultlessly. The King looked most impressive in his Coronation robes, and Queen Elizabeth wore a beautiful gown of ivory satin embroidered in gold with emblems of the British Isles and the Empire. Even the threatened rain stayed off so the huge crowds were able to enjoy the processions.

There were two unusual features to this Coronation. It was not customary for a Queen Dowager to attend the coronation of her successor, but Queen Mary elected to attend to give support to her son. As she and Queen Elizabeth passed each other in the abbey, Queen Mary curtsied in homage. In the royal box between Queen Mary and Princess Mary, the Princess Royal and sister of George VI, were the two little Princesses, Elizabeth and Margaret. The Indian princes, the peers and peeresses and representatives from around the world came to the coronation, for the king was still Emperor of India – the independence and partition of the country came in 1947 – so his oath was the same as his father's.

George VI proved himself a great king, and he passed on to his daughter, Elizabeth II, a true sense of duty. When he died the Cabinet wreath had a simple inscription: 'For Valour.' On a memorial in Yorkshire (a fitting place for a Duke of York) the message was simple:

TO THE GLORY OF GOD
AND IN MEMORY OF
GEORGE
KING
SERVANT OF HIS PEOPLE
1895 – 1952

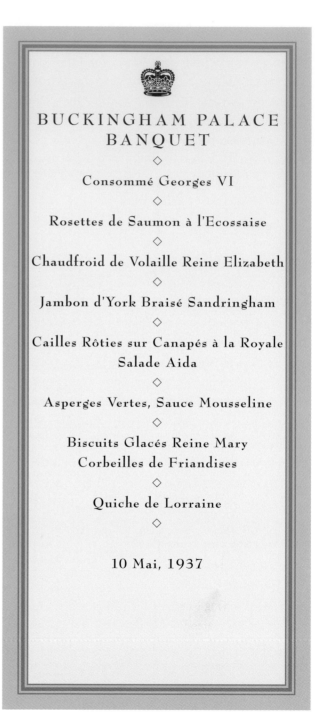

BUCKINGHAM PALACE
BANQUET
◇
Consommé Georges VI
◇
Rosettes de Saumon à l'Ecossaise
◇
Chaudfroid de Volaille Reine Elizabeth
◇
Jambon d'York Braisé Sandringham
◇
Cailles Rôties sur Canapés à la Royale
Salade Aida
◇
Asperges Vertes, Sauce Mousseline
◇
Biscuits Glacés Reine Mary
Corbeilles de Friandises
◇
Quiche de Lorraine
◇

10 Mai, 1937

Coronation banquet, 1937

The banquet for 10 May 1937 is one of several that were arranged in Coronation year. There are some differences between this menu and that for banquets arranged to mark the Coronation of the King's father, George V (see page 52). The dishes are simpler and although they have been given French names, they are mainly British. An interesting addition to the menu is Quiche de Lorraine, which would have been a very modern choice in 1937; quiches were first introduced to the general public in the late 1950s.

CONSOMMÉ GEORGES VI

GEORGE VI CONSOMMÉ

There is no classic recipe for a consommé called George VI, so I am giving the recipe for Chicken Consommé Edouard VII. It is likely that this might have been chosen as a tribute to the King's grandfather. Several garnishes are attributed to this soup and are included in the main recipe and the variations.

PREPARATION TIME: 25 MINUTES PLUS TIME TO PREPARE THE CONSOMMÉ

COOKING TIME: 15 MINUTES PLUS TIME TO COOK THE CONSOMMÉ

SERVES: 4–6

1.35 litres (2¼ pints) chicken consommé (see right)

3 level teaspoons arrowroot

salt and pepper

To garnish

truffles, neatly diced

cooked asparagus tips

3–4 tablespoons cooked chicken breast, finely diced

3–4 tablespoons port wine

Pour 1.2 litres (2 pints) of the consommé into a saucepan; blend the arrowroot with the remaining consommé. Add to the saucepan. Stir as the mixture comes to the boil and thickens. Season to taste.

Just before serving add the garnish and port wine then heat and serve.

Variations

Some recipes suggest that the consommé is delicately flavoured with curry. Portions of chicken loaf were sometimes added as garnish.

Other recipes do not thicken the consommé with arrowroot but garnish it with 3–4 tablespoons cooked long grain rice.

Small puff pastry cases, filled with chicken purée were served as an accompaniment.

Chicken Consommé

It is essential that a consommé is full of flavour, and before serving it must be quite clear. Although a whole chicken produces a good consommé it is even better if you use chicken stock produced from the carcass of a chicken instead of water.

Cut a small chicken into joints – the smaller the better, so the maximum flavour is extracted. Cover with 1.8 litres (3 pints) chicken stock or water and add salt and pepper to taste. One whole onion and a carrot can be added with 1–2 fresh bay leaves plus a small sprig of rosemary, but these are not essential. Cover the pan and simmer steadily for 2½–3 hours. Strain the liquid through several thicknesses of muslin placed over a sieve.

For maximum clarity, return the liquid to a saucepan and add the lightly whisked whites and shells of 2 eggs. Simmer for 10 minutes then strain again. Any minute particles of food will adhere to the whites and shells.

Serve as the recipe above.

Arrowroot is a thickener that does not spoil the clarity of a liquid.

ROSETTES DE SAUMON À L'ECOSSAISE

ROSETTES OF SCOTCH SALMON

This is a simple but delicious way of serving Scottish salmon for a special occasion. The term 'rosettes' would describe the presentation of the fish, usually given the French term *médallions*.

PREPARATION TIME: 35 MINUTES

COOKING TIME: COURT BOUILLON 15 MINUTES; SALMON 8–10 MINUTES

SERVES: 4

Court bouillon

300 ml (½ pint) dry white wine

300 ml (½ pint) water

I medium onion, sliced

I medium carrot, sliced

I sprig of parsley

I small sprig of lemon thyme

I tablespoon olive oil

salt and pepper

Rosettes of salmon

5 x 175 g (6 oz) salmon steaks (slices)

150 ml (¼ pint) double cream, whipped

2 teaspoons lemon juice

25 g (I oz) caviar

To garnish

100 g (3½ oz) smoked salmon, sliced and cut into strips

cucumber slices

lemon slices

Hollandaise Sauce (see page 35)

Put the ingredients for the court bouillon into a fish kettle or large shallow saucepan. Bring to the boil, cover and simmer gently for 15 minutes, then strain.

Return the liquid to the pan, add the salmon and simmer for 8–10 minutes or until the fish is just cooked but unbroken. Remove the pan from the heat. Take out one piece of fish, skin and bone this, and pound jus until smooth. Mix with the cream, lemon juice and salt and pepper.

Carefully take out the 4 salmon steaks from the pan, drain well, remove the centre bones and skin then form the fish into neat rounds. Place on a serving dish. Pipe or spoon the salmon cream in the centre and top with caviar. Arrange strips of smoked salmon, cucumber and lemon slices around the salmon and add spoonfuls of hollandaise sauce. Serve hot with new potatoes and fresh peas or cold with salads.

Variation

Use one of the inexpensive kinds of mock caviar.

CHAUDFROID DE VOLAILLE REINE ELIZABETH

CHICKEN IN CHAUDFROID SAUCE

The use of the word 'chaudfroid' indicates that the coating sauce over the food was first hot and then cold. When chicken was coated this was achieved by making a velouté sauce, adding flavour and a creamy appearance with the addition of a little mayonnaise and cream after first making sure that the mixture was sufficiently stiff by the addition of gelatine. Chaudfroid sauce on chicken and fish was considered very 'haute cuisine' in the 1930s.

PREPARATION TIME: 35 MINUTES PLUS TIME FOR THE COATING TO SET

COOKING TIME: 12–15 MINUTES

SERVES: 6

Velouté sauce

25 g (1 oz) butter

25 g (1 oz) plain flour

300 ml (1½ pint) chicken stock well clarified and strongly flavoured

Additions

1½ level teaspoons powder gelatine or 1–2 leaves (depending on size) of gelatine

2 tablespoons Mayonnaise (see page 129)

2 tablespoons double cream

6 cooked chicken breasts, free from skin and bone

To garnish

black and green olives, cut into neat pieces

diamond-shaped pieces of red pepper

Heat the butter in a saucepan, stir in the flour then gradually add three-quarters of the stock. Bring to the boil and stir over a low heat until thickened. Meanwhile, soak the gelatine in the remaining cold stock for 3 minutes. Add to the hot sauce and stir over a low heat until the gelatine has dissolved.

Allow the jellied sauce to cool, then stir in the mayonnaise and cream. Rub through a sieve to give a very smooth mixture, then chill until it has the consistency of lightly set jelly.

Place the chicken portions on a wire rack with a dish underneath to catch any drips. Evenly coat the chicken with the chaudfroid mixture. A palette knife dipped in very hot water, then shaken dry but used while hot, gives a smooth coating. Leave until the coating has almost set then arrange the garnish over the chicken.

Serve well chilled with various salads.

Variation

Aspic jelly was widely used in the 1930s, and another version of chaudfroid sauce was made by mixing the velouté sauce with 150 ml (¼ pint) liquid chicken aspic and omitting the mayonnaise and cream.

JAMBON D'YORK BRAISÉ SANDRINGHAM

BRAISED YORK HAM

York ham, a prime English meat, is cured by a splendid method that gives a delicious, mild taste. The ham is dry-salted and then smoked. After this it is matured for several months. Braised ham was very popular in the early and mid-1900s. The inclusion of the word Sandringham is a tribute to one of the royal homes but it may also refer to the delicious vegetables used in braising, which may have come from the estate.

PREPARATION TIME: 35 MINUTES PLUS POSSIBLE OVERNIGHT SOAKING

COOKING TIME: SIMMERING AS METHOD PLUS 45 MINUTES BRAISING

SERVES: ALLOW ABOUT 225–300 G (8–10 OZ) UNCOOKED HAM PER PERSON

joint of York ham

1–2 teaspoons pepper or peppercorns

To braise

8 shallots, halved

8 young carrots, thickly sliced

1 small celery heart, neatly diced

4–8 medium tomatoes, skinned and left whole

1 young turnip, finely diced

225 ml (7½ fl oz) Madeira or red wine

1 tablespoon chopped parsley

2 teaspoons chopped thyme

salt and pepper

To glaze

about 3 tablespoons demerara sugar, depending on the size of the joint

Weigh the ham before soaking. Although York ham has a mild taste compared to other hams and bacon, many people like to soak the joint over night in cold water to remove some of the salt taste. After soaking, strain away the soaking liquid.

Put the ham in a large pan with cold water to cover. Vegetables are used in braising, so there is no need to add any at this stage. Add a little pepper or peppercorns.

Calculate the cooking time. Allow 20 minutes per 450 g (1 lb) and 20 minutes over – for example, a 2.7 kg (6 lb) ham would take 2 hours 20 minutes. When braising, deduct 40 minutes for the oven cooking time. Simmer the ham gently; it should be almost cooked. After this stage lift the ham out of the water, then cut away the skin.

To braise, put the vegetables into the bottom of a deep braising pan or casserole. Add the Madeira or red wine, herbs and a little salt and pepper. Place the joint of ham on top of the vegetables and tightly cover the pan or casserole. Cook in a preheated oven, 190°C (375°F), Gas Mark 5, for 45 minutes. The ham should be perfectly tender at this stage. Remove the piece of ham from the container and place on an ovenproof platter.

Score the fat in a neat design and press the brown sugar over the fat. Put it back into the oven (uncovered) for 10 minutes or under a preheated grill to caramelize the sugar. Serve hot or cold with vegetables or salad. If serving hot the vegetables used in braising can be arranged around the ham.

Variation

The cooking time above refers to tender prime York ham on the bone. For other hams check the timing carefully: the joint may need another 5–10 minutes per 450 g (1 lb).

CAILLES RÔTIS SUR CANAPÉS À LA ROYALE

ROAST QUAIL ON CANAPÉS À LA ROYALE

In this banquet, as in the Coronation banquet of George V (see page 52), quail have been included on the menu. The small birds in this dish are boned, roasted and served on fried crisp croûtes, spread with foie gras to turn them into canapés.

PREPARATION TIME: 25 MINUTES

COOKING TIME: 15–21 MINUTES, DEPENDING ON SIZE, PLUS 25 MINUTES FOR
 MADEIRA SAUCE

SERVES: 4

8 quails, boned

50 g (2 oz) butter, melted

salt and pepper

Canapés

8 small slices of bread

25 g (1 oz) butter

2 tablespoons sunflower oil

175 g (6 oz) foie gras

To garnish

Madeira Sauce (see page 55)

watercress

Brush the small birds with the butter and season with salt and pepper. Roast in a preheated oven, 220°C (425°F), Gas Mark 7, for 15–21 minutes.

Meanwhile, cut the bread into pieces exactly the same size as the quails. Heat the butter and oil in a frying pan, fry the croûtons and put them on a serving dish. Spread with foie gras and top with the birds.

Pour the sauce around the birds immediately before serving so it does not soften the canapés, then add the watercress.

Variations

Instead of fried slices of bread use puff pastry, shaped as the quails, and cooked until well-risen and crisp. Top with foie gras then the quail.

Use the more economical Chicken Liver Pâté on page 57 instead of foie gras.

SALADE AIDA

AIDA SALAD

In spite of an Egyptian-sounding name, the ingredients in this salad are all readily available in Britain. The endive included in the salad is the curly green salad vegetable. The name is sometimes given to chicory.

PREPARATION TIME: 20 MINUTES

COOKING TIME: ABOUT 25 MINUTES

SERVES: 4–6

4 medium globe artichokes

4 large eggs

4 medium tomatoes, skinned

1 large or 2 small green peppers, deseeded

1 endive head

Dressing

3 tablespoons virgin olive oil

1 tablespoon sesame seed oil, or more olive oil

1 tablespoon white wine vinegar

1 tablespoon sherry vinegar

1–2 teaspoons Dijon mustard

1 teaspoon caster sugar

salt and pepper

Cook the artichokes in salted water until just tender; strip away the leaves and chokes, leaving just the bottoms. Cut these into matchstick shapes. Hard-boil the eggs and shell them. Chop the whites and yolks separately.

Halve the skinned tomatoes, remove the seeds and cut the pulp into narrow strips the same size as the artichokes. Cut the peppers into strips.

Shred the endive, put it into one large salad bowl or several individual ones. Top with the artichoke, tomato and green pepper strips.

Make the dressing by mixing the ingredients together. Spoon over the endive mixture then top with the chopped egg whites and yolks.

Variation

Add 2 teaspoons balsamic vinegar to the dressing in place of the same amount of wine or sherry vinegar.

ASPERGES VERTES, SAUCE MOUSSELINE

GREEN ASPARAGUS WITH MOUSSELINE SAUCE

It is interesting to note that green asparagus was chosen for the banquet because in 1937 people would have been more inclined to choose asparagus with green tips but whitish stems.

Mousseline sauce has a lighter texture than hollandaise sauce and is a perfect partner for asparagus.

PREPARATION TIME: 25 MINUTES

COOKING TIME: 20 MINUTES

SERVES: 4

1 large or 2 small bundles of green asparagus

Mousseline sauce

2 egg yolks

1 tablespoon lemon juice or white wine vinegar, or to taste

25 g (1 oz) butter, at room temperature

pinch of grated or ground nutmeg

3 tablespoons double cream, lightly whipped

salt and pepper

Cook the asparagus as described on page 34.

Mousseline sauce is made like Hollandaise Sauce (see page 35) but is easier to prepare because much less butter is used. Put the egg yolks, salt and pepper with the lemon juice or vinegar into the top of a double saucepan or basin over hot, but not boiling, water and whisk until thick and creamy. Cut the butter into small pieces and gradually whisk into the egg mixture. When thick, stir in the nutmeg and whisk as the sauce cools slightly. Fold in the whipped cream. Taste and adjust the seasoning. Serve warm or cold.

BISCUITS GLACÉS REINE MARY

BISCUIT ICE QUEEN MARY

There were several ways of making biscuit ices at this period. In some recipes individual moulds were lined with different kinds of sweet biscuits or with thin ice cream wafers, then filled with the ice cream mixture and frozen. In this particular presentation I have used a recipe for brandy snaps and made the thin biscuits into cup shapes to hold the ice cream.

The recipe given here is a classic one for ice cream and one of the best. It is made with uncooked eggs; in 1937, of course, chickens were not battery reared so there was less possibility of infection.

PREPARATION TIME: ICE CREAM 15 MINUTES PLUS FREEZING TIME; BRANDY
    SNAPS 20 MINUTES

COOKING TIME: ICE CREAM NO COOKING; BRANDY SNAP CUPS 8–9 MINUTES

SERVES: ICE CREAM 4–5; BRANDY SNAP CUPS 12–15

Ice cream

2 large eggs

50 g (2 oz) icing sugar, sifted

¼– ½ teaspoon vanilla extract

300 ml (½ pint) double cream

Brandy snap cups

50 g (2 oz) butter

50 g (2 oz) caster sugar

2 level tablespoons golden syrup

50 g (2 oz) plain flour (see method)

To decorate

crystallized rose and violet petals

alpine strawberries

Ice Cream

Put the eggs, sugar and vanilla extract into a mixing bowl. Whisk until thick and creamy. Pour the cream into another bowl and whip until just thick; do not over-whip because this makes the ice cream too solid.

Fold the whisked eggs and sugar into the cream. In a chef's kitchen in the 1930s, the mixture would be put into a manual ice cream maker, but this mixture freezes perfectly in a container in a freezer.

Brandy Snap Cups

Lightly grease 2–3 large baking sheets or line them with baking paper. Put the butter, sugar and golden syrup into a saucepan and allow to melt. Take out 1 teaspoon of flour from the 50 g (2 oz) – this gives the right amount to ensure a perfect consistency – and stir the flour into the melted ingredients. Put teaspoons of the mixture on to the sheets, leaving a space of about 7.5 cm (3 inches) around each biscuit.

Put one sheet of brandy snaps in a preheated oven, 160°C (325°F), Gas Mark 3, and cook for 8–9 minutes or until golden brown. Meanwhile, grease the base of small cups or glasses. Allow the biscuits to cool on the baking sheet for 2 minutes so they begin to stiffen. Lift the first biscuit off the sheet and press it around the base of the cup or glass. Continue like this until the biscuits harden, then gently remove from the cups or glasses. Put the next batch of biscuits into the oven and continue as above.

Serve the ice cream in the biscuit shapes and decorate.

Note: store the biscuit shapes in an airtight tin away from other biscuits.

Variations

The ice cream can be flavoured with a fruit purée. Allow 150 ml (¼ pint) strawberry, raspberry or other fruit purée to the basic recipe.

The brandy snap mixture can be flavoured with 1 teaspoon brandy or ½ teaspoon ground ginger.

Corbeilles de Friandises

These are similar to the petits fours described on page 59.

QUICHE DE LORRAINE

QUICHE LORRAINE

The early recipes for this savoury flan included a thin bread dough instead of pastry. Over the years the bread dough was changed to pastry and the filling began to include cheese and/or bacon or ham.

PREPARATION TIME: 30 MINUTES

COOKING TIME: 50–55 MINUTES

SERVES: 6

Pastry

175 g (6 oz) plain flour

pinch of salt

100 g (3½ oz) butter

cold water to bind

Filling

little egg white

150 g (5 oz) Gruyère cheese, grated

25 g (1 oz) Parmesan cheese, grated

2 eggs

3 egg yolks

300 ml (½ pint) double cream

salt and pepper

Sift the flour and salt, rub in the butter and add enough cold water to bind. If time permits wrap the pastry and let it stand for 30 minutes. Roll out and line a 23 cm (9 inch) flan tin or a flan ring on an upturned baking sheet. Put the flan in a preheated oven, 200°C (400°F), Gas Mark 6, and bake blind (see page 149). Remove from the oven. Brush egg white over the pastry to seal it and prevent the filling soaking in.

Sprinkle the cheeses over the the pastry. Whisk together the eggs, egg yolks and cream, season to taste with salt and pepper and strain over the cheese. Bake for 35–40 minutes or until the filling is firm at 160°C (325°F) Gas Mark 3. Serve hot or cold.

Variations

Fry or grill 4–5 rashers of bacon until crisp and add to the filling.

Use milk or half milk and half cream (single or double).

1937

CORONATION TEA PARTIES

Street parties were held to celebrate the Coronation of George VI and Queen Elizabeth. At the time of the Coronation the worries and arguments that had come with the abdication of Edward VIII had passed, and most people had become interested in the new royals and their family life.

By 1937 gas and electric cookers had become efficient, allowing good control of heat, so people felt confident enough to bake a good selection of cakes and pastries, and there was increasing interest in learning about French pastries. Many of the Coronation tea parties were organized in aid of charity, and they gave women an opportunity to show off their baking skills.

The pastries in the menu – the chocolate eclairs, choux, mille feuilles and so on – would be similar to those made for the banquets of Edward VII and George V.

THE MENU
SANDWICHES
SCONES WITH CREAM AND JAM (SEE PAGE 152)
CHERRY CAKE
GENOA CAKE
RAISIN CAKE
SEED CAKE
CHOCOLATE ECLAIRS
PRALINE CHOUX
MILLE FEUILLES
CREAM HORNS
MAIDS OF HONOUR
FRANGIPANE TARTLETS

SANDWICHES

These should be as varied and imaginative as possible. Be generous with the amount of filling and make sure the sandwiches do not dry out. Cover with clingfilm and store in the refrigerator until just before serving. Have a selection of white, brown and wholemeal breads.

Afternoon tea sandwiches should be small and it is considered correct to cut off the crusts. You may care to cut them into interesting shapes, such as hearts and diamonds. If you use half brown and half white bread for each sandwich you can achieve a colourful ribbon effect.

Avoid very moist fillings, such as sliced tomatoes, these could make the bread soggy. Make sure lettuce and other salad greens are finely shredded. Allow 3 to 4 small sandwiches per person.

CHERRY CAKE

It seemed that everyone wanted to make a perfect cherry cake in the late 1930s, generally for a special Coronation tea party. The trouble was that in most cases the cherries sank down in the cake.

Some people wash off the lovely sticky coating on the cherries with cold water then dry them well. However, the cherries lose so much moisture if you do this that I prefer to use a very small amount of raising agent and slow baking so that the cherries remain moist and sticky. Do not expect the cake to rise much.

PREPARATION TIME: 25 MINUTES

COOKING TIME: 1¾ HOURS

SERVES: 8

175 g (6 oz) butter

175 g (6 oz) caster sugar

3 large eggs, whisked

225 g (8 oz) plain flour with 1 level teaspoon baking powder

175–225 g (6–8 oz) glacé cherries, halved

Cream the butter and sugar until soft and light, then gradually beat in the eggs. Sift the flour and baking powder and mix with the cherries. Fold the mixture gently but thoroughly into the creamed mixture. Do not add any liquid.

Spoon into a greased and floured or lined 18 cm (7 inch) cake tin and bake in a preheated oven, 150°C (300°F), Gas Mark 2, for 1¾ hours or until firm to the touch.

Allow to cool for 5–10 minutes in the cake tin, then carefully turn out and place on a wire rack.

Variations

Bake in a 20 cm (8 inch) cake tin for barely 1½ hours.

Cherry Almond Cake

Use only 175 g (6 oz) plain flour with 1 level teaspoon baking powder plus 85 g (3 oz) ground almonds. Bake as before.

Either version of the cake can be topped with glacé icing (see page 73) and decorated with glacé cherries.

GENOA CAKE

<small>PREPARATION TIME: 25 MINUTES</small>

<small>COOKING TIME: 1½ HOURS</small>

<small>SERVES: 8</small>

175 g (6 oz) butter

175 g (6 oz) caster sugar

1 teaspoon grated lemon rind

4 large eggs, whisked

225 g (8 oz) plain flour with 1 level teaspoon baking powder

50 g (2 oz) mixed candied peel, chopped

225 g (8 oz) mixed dried fruit

1 tablespoon caster sugar, to top

Cream the butter, sugar and lemon rind until soft and light. Gradually beat in the eggs. If the mixture shows signs of curdling, fold in a little of the flour.

Sift the flour and baking powder, mix with the peel and fruit and stir into the creamed mixture.

Spoon into a greased and floured or lined 20 cm (8 inch) cake tin. Top the mixture with the caster sugar and bake in a preheated oven, 160°C (325°F), Gas Mark 3, for 1½ hours, or until firm to the touch. Allow to cool for 5–10 minutes in the cake tin then turn out on to a wire rack.

Raisin Cake

Omit the peel and mixed fruit and use 300 g (10 oz) seedless raisins. Deseed and chop these finely if they are large.

Seed or Seedy Cake

Omit the peel and dried fruit in the Genoa Cake. Add 2 teaspoons caraway seeds to the plain mixture.

Spoon into the cake tin, then before baking top with 1 tablespoon caster sugar mixed with 1 teaspoon caraway seeds. This cake should be cooked within 1 hour 20–25 minutes.

SOUVENIR of the CORONATION of their Majesties KING GEORGE VI & QUEEN ELIZABETH.

CHOCOLATE ECLAIRS

By 1937 these delicate pastries were becoming a great favourite in Britain. Many people were nervous about making choux pastry until they found that it was really quite simple. Oven temperatures are important. Make sure that the oven is thoroughly preheated, and if your oven is on the slow side, raise the heat slightly.

PREPARATION TIME: 30 MINUTES

COOKING TIME: 20–25 MINUTES

MAKES: 12–18

Choux pastry

150 ml (¼ pint) water

50 g (2 oz) butter

65 g (2½ oz) plain flour

pinch of salt

1 teaspoon sugar

2 eggs

Filling

225 ml (7½ fl oz) double cream, whipped

25 g (1 oz) icing sugar, sifted, or caster sugar

few drops vanilla extract (see page 37)

Chocolate icing

175 g (6 oz) icing sugar, sifted

2–3 teaspoons cocoa powder (see Variations)

water to bind

Put the water and butter in a good-sized saucepan and heat gently until the butter melts. Remove from the heat. Sift the flour with the salt and sugar into a bag or on to a sheet of greaseproof paper so it is easy to tip into the saucepan.

After adding the flour, stir well to mix all the ingredients. Return to the cooker over a gentle heat and stir continually until the flour mixture forms a ball and leaves the sides of the saucepan clear. Take off the heat and leave to cool.

Whisk the eggs briskly then beat gradually into the flour mixture to give a sticky texture that stands in soft peaks. You may not need quite all the second egg.

To make eclairs, lightly grease 1 or 2 baking sheets and dust with a very little flour. With your forefinger or the end of a wooden spoon, mark 12–18 straight lines of equal length. Put the choux pastry mixture into a cloth piping bag fitted with a 1.25 cm (½ inch) plain nozzle. Pipe fingers of the pastry on the sheets.

Bake in a preheated oven, 200°C (400°F), Gas Mark 6, for 20–25 minutes. Remove from the oven and place away from draughts. Pierce the sides of the buns with the tip of a sharp knife to allow the steam to escape. Place on a wire rack to cool.

When the buns are cold, split and fill with the cream mixed with sugar to taste and the vanilla.

Mix the ingredients for the chocolate icing, spread it over the top of the éclairs and leave to set.

Variations

Make miniature eclairs that are half-sized fingers and bake for 10–14 minutes only.

Instead of cocoa powder, melt 50 g (2 oz) plain chocolate in a basin over hot water. Cool, then add the icing sugar, 2 teaspoons melted butter and enough cold water to bind.

PRALINE CHOUX

These small choux are filled with a sweet, nutty mixture.

PREPARATION TIME: 25 MINUTES

COOKING TIME: 30–35 MINUTES

MAKES: 12

Choux pastry (see left)

Filling

100 g (3½ oz) praline or nut brittle toffee, crushed

150 ml (¼ pint) double cream, whipped

1 teaspoon rum, brandy or orange juice

Topping

about 25 g (1 oz) icing sugar, sifted

Make the choux pastry as described for chocolate eclairs. Spoon or pipe 12 rounds well apart on a greased baking sheet. Bake in a preheated oven, 200°C (400°F), Gas Mark 6, allowing 30–35 minutes or until well-risen, golden and firm. Remove from the oven and place away from draughts. Pierce each bun with the tip of a knife to allow the steam to escape. Lift on to a wire rack. When quite cold, split the buns.

Blend the filling ingredients together, put into the buns and top with the icing sugar.

Variations

To make cream choux, fill the buns with sweetened whipped cream instead of the praline mixture.

To make praline profiteroles, prepare 24–30 small choux but bake for 15–20 minutes.

MILLE FEUILLES

Home-made puff pastry has a wonderfully light texture and a rich flavour. It takes time to make and should be kept cool during the making process. This was not easy in the 1930s, when relatively few people owned a refrigerator. 'Mille feuilles' means a 'thousand layers', and although that may be an exaggeration it should have many.

PREPARATION TIME: 1 HOUR PLUS TIME TO STAND

COOKING TIME: 15 MINUTES

MAKES: 8–10

225 g (8 oz) unsalted butter, weight when water extracted
225 g (8 oz) plain flour (see Variations)
pinch of salt
2 teaspoons lemon juice
ice cold water to mix
Filling
300 ml (½ pint) double cream, whipped
Topping
Glacé Icing (see page 73)

In the 1930s, the butter would have been wrapped in a soft cloth or piece of gauze and squeezed over a basin to extract any surplus moisture. After doing this, check the weight and form the butter into a neat oblong.

Sift the flour and salt into a mixing bowl, add the lemon juice and enough water to make an elastic pliable dough. Roll out to a neat oblong.

Place the butter in the centre of the dough. Bring up the bottom third of the dough to cover the butter and bring down the top third of the dough to cover this. Turn the dough, seal the ends, then depress the dough at intervals. Roll out again and repeat the folding process. This has to be done seven times, but the dough must be allowed to rest several times.

Roll out the dough until it is about 1.25 cm (½ inch) thick. Cut it into 16–20 equal-sized fingers. Trim the edges of these, which encourages the pastry to rise, and prick very lightly.

Put the pastries on baking sheets, which should be damped with cold water. Bake in a preheated oven, 220–230°C (425–450°F), Gas Mark 7–8, for 15 minutes or until firm. Lift on to a wire rack.

When cold, sandwich two fingers with the whipped cream and top with glacé icing.

Variations

Use strong (bread) flour instead of plain flour.

Fill the pastry with whipped cream mixed with lemon curd.

Roll the pastry until it is 2.5–3 cm (1–1¼ inch) thick. Bake as above, cool then split through the centre and sandwich the two layers together as above.

Cream Horns

The secret of perfect cream horns is to handle the puff pastry without stretching it. Pastry made with 225 g (8 oz) butter as for Mille Feuilles (see page 99) makes 12–18 cream horns.

Roll out the pastry until it is about 5 mm (¼ inch) thick. Cut it into strips about 2.5 cm (1 inch) wide and 28–30 cm (11–12 inch) long. Lightly grease cream horn tins and wind the strips around the tins, starting at the bottom ends. Moisten the edges and make certain that the strips overlap by 5 mm (¼ inch). Do not allow the pastry to come over the top of the tins, which would make it difficult to pull out the tins after baking. Cool for 30 minutes before baking.

Place the horns on one or more baking sheets with the joins touching the sheets and bake in a preheated oven, 220°C (425°F), Gas Mark 7, for 10 minutes. Remove from the oven, brush with lightly whisked egg white and dredge with caster sugar. Return to the oven for a further 10–15 minutes. Allow to cool for 5 minutes then carefully withdraw the tins and put the horns on a wire rack. When quite cold fill with jam or a thick fruit purée and top with whipped cream.

MAIDS OF HONOUR

It is believed that these tartlets were made by Anne Boleyn and her maids of honour to please Henry VIII. Sadly, they did not prevent poor Anne from being beheaded.

PREPARATION TIME: 35 MINUTES

COOKING TIME: 16–18 MINUTES

MAKES: 12–18

Sweet Shortcrust Pastry (see right)

Filling

50 g (2 oz) butter

50 g (2 oz) caster sugar

½ teaspoon grated lemon rind

175 g (6 oz) soft curd cheese

25 g (1 oz) ground almonds or fine cake crumbs

2 teaspoons brandy or orange flower water

Make the pastry, roll out and line 12–18 patty tins. Chill while you prepare the filling.

Cream the butter, sugar and lemon rind. Gradually beat in the remainder of the ingredients. Spoon into the pastry cases and bake in a preheated oven, 200°C (400°F), Gas Mark 6, for 16–18 minutes or until the pastry and filling are set. If necessary, reduce the oven temperature slightly for the last few minutes.

Variations

Puff pastry made with 150 g (5 oz) flour and 150 g (5 oz) butter was often used for these. In this case bake for 10 minutes at 220°C (425°F), Gas Mark 7, then lower the heat to 160° (325°F), Gas Mark 3, for the remainder of the time.

The filling can be topped with Glacé Icing (see page 73) and decorated with crystallized rose or violet petals.

FRANGIPANE TARTLETS

The filling in these sweet tartlet cases had been made by exclusive bakers for some time, but it was relatively unknown to home cooks until towards the end of the 1930s. The pastry is crisp and sweet. In the past a pinch of salt was added to all kinds of pastry.

PREPARATION TIME: 35 MINUTES

COOKING TIME: 15–18 MINUTES PLUS 10 MINUTES FOR THE FILLING

MAKES: 12–18

Filling

1 level tablespoon cornflour

225 ml (7½ fl oz) single cream or milk

2 eggs

25–50 g (1–2 oz) caster sugar (see method)

50 g (2 oz) ground almonds or crushed macaroons

Sweet shortcrust pastry

175 g (6 oz) plain flour

pinch of salt

100 g (3½ oz) butter

50g (2 oz) caster sugar

1 egg yolk

water to bind

2 tablespoons apricot jam

To decorate

icing sugar or **Glacé Icing** (see page 73)

glacé cherries and angelica

Blend the cornflour with the cream or milk. Pour into a saucepan and stir over a low heat until the mixture thickens. Remove from the heat. Beat in the eggs and add the sugar (use the smaller amount with macaroon crumbs). Return to a low heat and stir for 2–3 minutes. Remove from the heat. Lastly add the ground almonds or the macaroons. Allow to cool.

Sift the flour and salt into a bowl, rub in the butter, add the sugar and egg yolk. Mix thoroughly, then gradually add enough water to make a firm rolling consistency. Cover and chill for a short time, then roll out and line 12–18 patty tins. Chill again. Prick the base of each pastry case.

Bake the tartlet cases in a preheated oven, 200°C (400°F), Gas Mark 6, for 5 minutes only;, remove from the oven. Put a little jam in each pastry case then add the filling. Reduce the heat to 190°C (375°F), Gas Mark 5 and bake for a further 10–13 minutes or until the pastry and filling are firm. Remove from the tins on to a wire rack and leave until cold.

Either top with sifted icing sugar or a little glacé icing. Decorate with small pieces of glacé cherry and angelica leaves.

Variation

Frangipane Boats were a great favourite, and boat-shaped tins are readily available. Bake for a total of 10–12 minutes for the shallow shape.

ELIZABETH II

REIGNED FROM 1952

THE FUTURE QUEEN ELIZABETH II WAS BORN
IN BRUTON STREET, THE LONDON HOME OF
HER MATERNAL GRANDPARENTS, THE EARL
AND COUNTESS OF STRATHMORE, ON 26 APRIL 1926, A
COLD AND WINDY DAY. SHE WAS CHRISTENED
ELIZABETH ALEXANDRA MARY, AND HER FAMILY
CALLED HER LILIBET. THE DUKE WROTE TO HIS FATHER,
GEORGE V: 'YOU DON'T KNOW WHAT A TREMENDOUS
JOY IT IS TO ELIZABETH AND ME TO HAVE OUR LITTLE
GIRL. WE ALWAYS WANTED A CHILD TO MAKE OUR
HAPPINESS COMPLETE AND NOW IT HAS HAPPENED, IT
SEEMS SO WONDERFUL AND STRANGE.'

Early Years
1926-1931

ABOVE: Princess Elizabeth aged four wearing a party dress.

AT THE TIME OF HER BIRTH THERE WAS NO THOUGHT THAT ELIZABETH WOULD BECOME QUEEN, FOR HER UNCLE, THE PRINCE OF WALES, WAS YOUNG AND MIGHT WELL MARRY AND HAVE CHILDREN. HER PARENTS WERE DEVOTED TO THEIR BABY DAUGHTER, AND SO WERE KING GEORGE AND QUEEN MARY. THIS WAS SOMEWHAT SURPRISING, FOR THEY HAD BEEN STRICT AND RATHER AUSTERE PARENTS WITH THEIR OWN CHILDREN, BUT THEY SEEMED ALMOST BESOTTED WITH THEIR GRANDDAUGHTER.

The London home of the Yorks was 145 Piccadilly, very near Buckingham Palace, and Queen Mary sought many opportunities to see the baby, even sending her car round for the young Princess when she had guests for tea. Just over a year after her birth, the Duke and Duchess made an official visit to Australia and New Zealand, a journey undertaken by sea, and during their long absence the Princess stayed with the King and Queen at Buckingham Palace. King George was quite happy for the little girl to sit on his knee and pull his beard – something that had never happened with his own children.

To the delight of the public many pictures were published of the princess, and when she was three the first biography, *The Story of Princess Elizabeth*, appeared. After this other books were published, all proving to be extremely popular.

Winston Churchill stayed at Sandringham, a country home of the royal family, when Princess Elizabeth was just under two years old. He wrote: 'She perched on a little chair between the King and me, and the King gave her biscuits to eat and to feed his little dog, the King chortled with little jokes with her. After a game of bricks on the floor with the young equerry, she was fetched by her nurse, and made a perfectly sweet curtsy to the King and Queen and then to the company as she departed.'

When Elizabeth was four years old her sister, Margaret Rose, was born in August 1930. There is no doubt that the princesses grew up in a happy family atmosphere. The Duke of York was particularly anxious that they should have a more relaxed childhood than he had enjoyed, while the Duchess, who had been more fortunate in experiencing a happy childhood, wanted her children to have the same benefit. An important person joined the nursery staff soon after Margaret Rose was born.

Margaret McDonald, known as Bobo, was engaged as the nursery maid, and she was later appointed dresser to Princess Elizabeth, remaining with her until her death in September 1993. Over the years she became a true friend, and Elizabeth welcomed her commonsense and advice.

BELOW: A young Princess Elizabeth and her sister Princess Margaret sitting on the grass in the grounds of the Royal Lodge, Windsor,

Growing Up
1932–1938

ABOVE: A souvenir poster for the Coronation of King George VI, including pictures of Princess Elizabeth and Margaret.
RIGHT: Princess Elizabeth and Margaret, photographed with the penguins at London Zoo.

IN 1932 THE YORK FAMILY ACQUIRED A COUNTRY HOME, ROYAL LODGE, WINDSOR, WHERE THE TWO PRINCESSES ENJOYED COUNTRY LIFE. MANY PHOTOGRAPHS WERE PUBLISHED OF THE CHILDREN WITH THEIR DOGS AND PONIES, AND THEY WERE SHOWN HAVING FUN WITH THEIR PARENTS. IT SEEMED AN IDYLLIC EXISTENCE, BUT IT WAS A SOMEWHAT LONELY ONE, FOR THE CHILDREN HAD LITTLE CONTACT WITH OTHER YOUNG PEOPLE.

The Duchess of York supervised the education of her daughters and engaged a governess, Miss Marion Crawford, because there was no question of the Princesses attending a school. The happy existence continued until 1936 when life changed dramatically for the York family. On the death of George V, Edward, Prince of Wales, became Edward VIII, but before he could be crowned he abdicated. The Duke of York became George VI, and in December 1936 the

Princesses heard cheering outside their London home and voices calling for their father. It was then that Elizabeth realized that at some future time she would be Queen. 'Poor you,' her sister remarked, and the family moved into Buckingham Palace.

In view of the changed situation Queen Mary decided that her elder granddaughter should learn more about the history of Britain and of the British Empire, and she arranged for Sir Henry Marten, the Vice-Provost of Eton, to instruct Elizabeth. A French teacher was also appointed. Over the years Queen Mary took her granddaughter on various educational visits to historical places. George VI spent a great deal of time and effort on his duties as king, and his daughter watched and learned from his sense of duty and discipline.

When Princess Elizabeth was 13 years old she met Prince Philip for the first time. At the time Prince Philip, who was 18 years old, was at the Royal Naval College, Dartmouth, which the royal family were visiting. The Prince was deputed to show them around (see also page 111).

LEFT: Remembrance Day at the Cenotaph in London (left to right) Lieutenant Mountbatten (Duke of Edinburgh), Princess Elizabeth (Queen Elizabeth II) and King George VI.

Wartime
1939-1945

WHEN WAR WAS DECLARED ON
3 SEPTEMBER 1939 THE PRINCESSES
WERE ON THEIR USUAL HOLIDAY VISIT
TO BALMORAL. IT WAS ORIGINALLY
WIDELY BELIEVED THAT THE
PRINCESSES WOULD BE SENT TO SAFETY
IN CANADA, BUT THE QUEEN STATED
THAT, AS THE KING WOULD NOT LEAVE
BRITAIN, NEITHER WOULD SHE NOR
THEIR DAUGHTERS. THE KING AND
QUEEN SPENT THE WAR YEARS IN
LONDON AT BUCKINGHAM PALACE,
AND FOR MOST OF THIS TIME THE TWO
PRINCESSES WERE AT ROYAL LODGE,
WINDSOR, WITH SOME VISITS TO
WINDSOR CASTLE.

LEFT: Princess Elizabeth making her first radio broadcast, accompanied by her younger sister, Princess Margaret Rose.

RIGHT: Princess Elizabeth changing a lorry's wheel at an ATS Training Centre in her position as a Second Subaltern in the service.

On 13 October 1940 Princess Elizabeth made her first radio broadcast, speaking to the children who had been evacuated from their homes. In 1944 she made her first solo public appearance, attending a meeting of the governors of Queen Elizabeth Hospital for Children.

One of the highlights of these war years was the pantomime at Windsor Castle, in which the Princess took the role of the principal boy. During these years Elizabeth begged to be allowed to help the national effort. When she was 16 she enrolled in the youth service as a Sea Ranger, and when she was 18 she achieved her wish to serve

in the forces, when she became a member of the Auxiliary Transport Service (ATS).

VE day was on 8 May 1945, and the whole of Britain rejoiced. The two Princesses begged to be allowed to join the people in London, and they joined the crowds without being recognized.

Prince Philip, Duke of Edinburgh

1921 -

ABOVE: Princess Elizabeth and Prince Phillip, Duke of Edinburgh at Buckingham Palace shortly before their wedding.

THE EARLY LIFE OF PRINCE PHILIP WAS VERY DIFFERENT FROM THAT OF MOST ROYAL PRINCES, FOR IT WAS FULL OF UNCERTAINTY AND CHANGE. HE WAS BORN ON 10 JUNE 1921 ON CORFU. HIS MOTHER, PRINCESS ALICE, WAS A DAUGHTER OF PRINCE LOUIS BATTENBURG, AND HIS GRANDMOTHER, VICTORIA OF HESSE, WAS THE DAUGHTER OF QUEEN VICTORIA'S SECOND DAUGHTER, ALICE. HIS FATHER, PRINCE ANDREW OF GREECE AND DENMARK, WAS NOT WITH THE FAMILY, FOR HE HAD REJOINED HIS REGIMENT OF THE GREEK ARMY, WHICH WAS FIGHTING WHAT PROVED TO BE A LOSING BATTLE AGAINST THE TURKS.

As a result Constantine I, Prince Andrew's elder brother, was exiled and Prince Andrew was arrested and threatened with execution. Princess Alice sought help from her various royal connections, and the pleas of her younger brother, Lord Mountbatten, led George V to ask that a warship be sent to secure the Prince's release. The family, with Philip, who was then barely a year old, were taken to safety in Brindisi, and on to Paris, where they spent the next seven years.

Although Prince Philip was known as Philip of Greece, his ancestry on his grandfather's side was Danish. In 1863 the Greeks, who were without a monarch, approached Prince William of Denmark, the second son of Christian IX, to be their ruler. He reigned as George I, marrying Olga, a niece of Nicholas I of Russia in 1867. The royal couple worked hard for their adopted country and its people, but there were repeated attempts on the King's life, and he was eventually assassinated in 1913.

Prince Philip's family found other royal refugees in Paris, so as he grew he had plenty of company. Princess Alice and Prince Andrew began to lead quite separate lives and drifted apart, as the Princess opened a shop to help the family finances. At this time Philip was in the care of a British nanny and the household was run by a British housekeeper.

Philip's four elder sisters had married German aristocrats and now lived in that country, and it was decided that Philip should go to England and attend Cheam preparatory school. His uncle, the Marquess of Milford Haven, acted as his guardian. After attending Cheam Phillip went to Gordonstoun school in Scotland. The headmaster, Kurt Hahn, had founded a school in Germany but had been forced to leave that country by the Nazis. He opened the school in Scotland, and it soon achieved a high reputation.

When he was 18 years old Prince Philip went to the Royal Naval College, Dartmouth, and it was there that he had his first meeting with Princess Elizabeth. The handsome young man made a great impression on the 13-year-old princess.

On the outbreak of war Philip joined the Royal Navy, first seeing action in 1941 at Cape Matapan, after which he was mentioned in despatches for gallantry.

ABOVE: Prince Phillip, captain of the Windsor Park Team after they beat India during the Ascot week Polo tournament. The cup was presented by Queen Elizabeth II who is at his side.

Later the ship on which he served took part in the landings on Sicily. In 1944 he was posted to the Pacific for the war against Japan. When he was on leave in Britain he visited Windsor Castle and Buckingham Palace, and Princess Elizabeth wrote to him quite regularly.

After his marriage Prince Philip continued his naval career in Greenwich and then on active duty as first lieutenant of HMS *Chequers* in the Mediterranean. He was subsequently appointed to the command of the frigate HMS *Magpie*.

On the death of George VI Prince Philip gave up his naval career to support the queen in her royal duties, and throughout the years he has steadfastly fulfilled his role as her consort. The prince is patron or president of some 800 organizations with special emphasis on scientific and technological research. The Duke of Edinburgh's Award Scheme, which was started in 1956, helps young people between the ages of 15 and 25 to achieve their full potential in various fields. Since its inception more than two million young people in 50 countries have taken part in this challenging scheme.

Romance and Marriage

1947

PRINCESS ELIZABETH AND PRINCE PHILIP MET FROM TIME TO TIME DURING THE WAR, AND IN 1946, THE PRINCE PROPOSED. KING GEORGE WAS TOLD OF HIS DAUGHTER'S DESIRE TO MARRY BUT HE WANTED HER TO CONSIDER THE MATTER MORE CAREFULLY, AND HE PERSUADED PRINCESS ELIZABETH TO ACCOMPANY HIM, THE QUEEN AND PRINCESS MARGARET ON AN OFFICIAL VISIT TO SOUTH AFRICA. IT WAS DURING THIS TOUR THAT THE PRINCESS MADE A MEMORABLE BROADCAST ON THE OCCASION OF HER 21ST BIRTHDAY, WHEN SHE SPOKE OF HER DESIRE TO SERVE HER COUNTRY AND ITS PEOPLE.

The family returned to Britain, and consent was given to the wedding. The official engagement was announced on 9 July 1947, and crowds cheered the couple when they appeared on the balcony of Buckingham Palace.

The wedding took place at Westminster Abbey on 20 November 1947. Princess Elizabeth's dress – for which she had been granted extra clothing coupons – was designed by Norman Hartnell and shimmered with crystals and costume pearls. The occasion brought a wonderful touch of glamour to a nation that had endured the grey days of war and its aftermath. Just before the wedding it was announced that Prince Philip was to be known as the Duke of Edinburgh. The honeymoon was spent at the home of Prince Philip's uncle in Romsey.

The royal couple were due to live at Clarence House, but as that needed a considerable amount of renovation they lived for a time at Buckingham Palace. On her return from honeymoon the Princess embarked on the familiar round of public duties, and she continued with these, even when pregnant. On 24 November 1948 a son, Charles Philip Arthur George, was born at Buckingham Palace.

Prince Philip had taken up naval duties in Malta in 1949, where the Princess joined him and lived as an ordinary naval wife. Princess Anne Elizabeth Alice Louise was born at Clarence House on 15 August 1950.

It was at this time that the health of George VI began to deteriorate. In 1951 he underwent a major lung operation, and Princess Elizabeth represented him at the Trooping the Colour and during the official visits of the kings of Denmark and Norway.

After Christmas in England the Princess and the Duke of Edinburgh left on 31 January 1952 for a tour of Australia and New Zealand. Pictures on television and in the press showed George VI bidding the couple farewell, and it was obvious that he was incredibly frail. It had been arranged

that they would break their journey in Kenya, where they would see the hunting lodge that had been given them as a wedding present by the people of that country. It was while they were staying there that the news of the death of George VI was relayed to them. He had died peacefully in his sleep in the early hours of 6 February 1952 at Sandringham. Princess Elizabeth was now Queen Elizabeth II.

BELOW: Princess Elizabeth and Prince Phillip with their two children in the grounds of Clarence House, London.

The Year of Accession
1952

ABOVE: Princess Elizabeth is greeted by Winston Churchill on her return from Africa following the death of her father George VI.

QUEEN ELIZABETH FLEW BACK TO BRITAIN, ARRIVING AT HEATHROW ON 8 FEBRUARY 1952. FEW PEOPLE WILL FORGET THE PICTURES OF THE YOUNG QUEEN DRESSED IN BLACK, WALKING ALONE DOWN THE STEPS OF THE PLANE TO BE GREETED BY HER PRIME MINISTER, SIR WINSTON CHURCHILL, OTHER MINISTERS AND THE LEADER OF OPPOSITION, CLEMENT ATTLEE. PRINCE PHILIP WALKED BEHIND HIS WIFE, FOR IT WAS PROTOCOL THAT SHE MUST PRECEDE HIM ON ALL PUBLIC OCCASIONS. ON THAT EVENING CHURCHILL BROADCAST TO THE NATION — HE PAID TRIBUTE TO THE LATE KING AND RECALLED HIS YOUTH IN THE DAYS OF QUEEN VICTORIA.

On 11 February the three queens, Mary (mother of King George VI), Elizabeth (his widow, who throughout the years ahead would be known with great affection as the Queen Mother) and Elizabeth II, went to Westminster Hall to pay their respects to the late King, who was lying in state. His funeral took place on 15 February.

During the early part of 1952, thought was given to the official name of the royal house. In 1917, during the First World War, the royal family had decided to drop all references to Saxe-Coburg, derived from Prince Albert, and to be known simply as the House of Windsor. Prince Philip had adopted the name Mountbatten, and there was some debate whether this should be incorporated. The government decided against this and it was agreed that the Royal House of Windsor should remain the family name. It was also decided that Prince Philip should head the council responsible for planning the Coronation.

The new Queen's first public engagement was on Maundy Thursday (the Thursday before Good Friday) when she presented specially minted silver coins to the number of poor pensioners who totalled her age (then 25). On 5 June she rode in her first Trooping the Colour ceremony on the police horse, Winston, and later that month she opened Royal Ascot. Shortly afterwards she visited Edinburgh to thank the people of Scotland for their loyal affection. On 1 July she visited members of the British North Greenland Expedition before they sailed for the Arctic.

On 2 November, accompanied by Prince Philip, the Queen formally opened the first new parliamentary session of her reign. On Christmas Day she broadcast her first message to Britain, saying: 'Let us set out to build a truer knowledge of ourselves and our fellow men, to work for tolerance and understanding among the nations and to use the tremendous forces of science and learning for the betterment of man's lot upon the earth.'

RIGHT: Queen Elizabeth II and Prince Phillip, Duke of Edinburgh (left) taking a salute during a Trooping of the Colour ceremony outside Buckingham Palace, London.

Events of 1952

ABOVE: American actress Elizabeth Taylor with her new husband Michael Wilding after their wedding at Caxton Hall in London.

January

British headmasters criticize the new GCE (General Certificate of Education) as being too hard.

Winston Churchill has talks in Washington with President Truman and agrees that US forces should use British bases for the common defence of the two countries.

The British government announces new austerity measures, including NHS charges and cuts in imports.

February

The United Nations holds its first session in New York.

Actress Elizabeth Taylor marries Michael Wilding in London.

Identity cards, which had been issued during the war, are finally abolished.

Churchill announces that Britain has an atomic bomb.

March

The USA doubles 'defence aid' to Britain to a total of £214 million.

Over 20,000 NHS doctors get a rise of £500 a year, backdated to 1948.

Oscars are awarded to Vivien Leigh as best actress for *A Streetcar Named Desire* and to Humphrey Bogart as best actor in *The African Queen*.

More than 200 people are killed and 2,500 injured as a tornado sweeps along the Mississippi valley.

Oxford win the Boat Race in blizzard conditions.

April

General Eisenhower asks to be relieved of the command of NATO to seek nomination as the Republican candidate in the presidential elections later in the year.

The cheese ration is cut to 25 g (1 oz) a week.

President Truman marks the official end of the Second World War in the Pacific by signing the peace treaty; 49 states (excluding the Soviet Union) join in recognizing Japanese sovereignty.

May

The jet era begins when the first scheduled Comet flight leaves London for Johannesburg.

In the House of Commons all parties approve moves to ensure that women who do the same job as men receive equal pay; legislation is to be introduced in stages.

The Queen gives permission to Benjamin Britten to write a coronation opera about Queen Elizabeth I and the Earl of Essex.

June

It is announced that the 'iron curtain' will be lowered between West Berlin and the Soviet Zone and that all West Germans will need special permits to enter the Eastern Zone.

Denis Compton makes his first century in cricket.

Chris Chataway runs 2 miles (3.2 km) in a record time of 8 minutes 55.6 seconds.

In London it is announced that zebra crossings will be marked by blinking orange beacons.

July

The 17-year-old American, Maureen Connolly, known as Little Mo, wins the Ladies Singles at Wimbledon.

In London people bid farewell to the last tram, which ran from Woolwich to New Cross.

The US liner United States crosses the Atlantic in a record 3 days, 10 hours, 40 minutes.

Findings from the 1951 census reveal that one in three houses in Britain lacks a bath and one in 20 has no piped water.

August

The Olympics open in Helsinki and are dominated by the Czech runner Emil Zatopek; the show-jumping team wins Britain's only gold medal.

Freak thunderstorms in north Devon lead to disastrous floods in which thousands of people are made homeless and several die.

For the first time, Surrey wins the county cricket championship outright.

A British Canberra bomber plane breaks all flying records when it flies from Aldergrove, Northern Ireland, to Gander, Newfoundland, and back within 8 hours.

September

Field Marshall Sir William Slim is appointed Governor-General of Australia.

Charlie Chaplin, visiting London for the first time in 23 years, is investigated in the USA as a 'subversive'.

The Yorkshire cricketer, Freddie Trueman, aged 21, wins the Cricket Writers' Club trophy as best young cricketer of 1952.

October

British troops fly to Nairobi as the government of Kenya declares a state of emergency over the Mau Mau terrorists.

In England's worst railway disaster, 112 people are killed at Harrow when three trains collide.

Britain's first atomic bomb is tested successfully off the northwest coast of Australia.

November

Dwight D. Eisenhower is elected as the 34th president of the USA.

Maria Callas, the Greek soprano, wins praise for her London debut in Bellini's *Norma* at the Royal Opera House, Covent Garden.

Jomo Kenyatta is charged with being head of the Mau Mau in Kenya.

Agatha Christie's play *The Mousetrap* opens at the Ambassadors Theatre and a critic says 'it has a fair chance of success'.

December

Charlie Chaplin's new film *Limelight*, starring Chaplin, Claire Bloom and Buster Keaton, opens to mixed reviews.

President-elect Eisenhower meets General MacArthur in Korea to discuss plans for ending the war.

Smog in London causes the deaths of more than 2,000 people.

ABOVE: American tennis player Maureen Connolly holding the women's singles trophy after beating fellow American Louise Brough at the Wimbledon Lawn Tennis Championships.

Coronation year

1953

ABOVE: Crowds waking up in the rain after spending all night sleeping in Trafalgar Square before the Coronation.

EVEN WITH THE MANY EXTRA ENGAGEMENTS ASSOCIATED WITH HER CORONATION, THE QUEEN CARRIED OUT THE EXACTING DUTIES REQUIRED OF THE REIGNING MONARCH. ONE SAD EVENT MARRED THE EXCITEMENT AND HAPPINESS OF 1953: ON 25 MARCH QUEEN MARY DIED AT HER HOME, MARLBOROUGH HOUSE. THE FUNERAL TOOK PLACE ON 31 MARCH, AND THE CROWDS THAT GATHERED WERE AN INDICATION OF THE WIDESPREAD RESPECT FELT BY THE BRITISH PEOPLE FOR THIS DIGNIFIED LADY.

In April the Queen launched the new royal yacht *Britannia*, a magnificent ship that was much admired and that would give great delight to the royal family for many decades to come. The Queen's love of horses was well known, and she enjoyed time at the Olympic Horse Trials at Badminton with Princess Margaret.

Towards the end of 1953 the Queen had to consider the problem facing Princess Margaret, who was in love with Group Captain Peter Townsend, a former equerry to her father and now the Comptroller of the Queen Mother's household. They wished to marry, but Townsend had been divorced. Princess Margaret herself decided this marriage could not take place.

The Coronation was due to take place on 2 June, and the day before came the thrilling news of the conquest of Mount Everest on 29 May by the New Zealander, Edmund Hillary, and Sherpa Tenzing Norgay, members of an expedition led by John Hunt.

Like all coronation ceremonies, that of Elizabeth II entailed much thought and planning. The arrangements for coronations through the centuries have been overseen by the Earl Marshal of England, a hereditary office held by the Duke of Norfolk, chief member of the Coolege of Arms. The Earl Marshal and the Heralds with the Pursuivants have from the earliest times been the authorities on state ceremonial and would have the final word in all matters of protocol. In addition, the Coronation Council (or Commission) under the chairmanship of the Duke of Edinburgh, which had been set up in 1952, dealt with many other important aspects of the great event. The Duke of Norfolk was deputy chairman, and members included the Prime Minister, Lord Chancellor and Lord Chamberlain. It was essential that authorities from the Commonwealth were involved in the planning for they had to decide who would attend the ceremony and the troops they would send to be part of the Coronation parade.

The Queen and her advisers wanted the Coronation to be of great splendour, especially as it would be televised for the first time and filmed for people around the world. Westminster Abbey was closed for months so that 7,000 tiered seats could be erected. All the ceremonial chairs were re-upholstered, chandeliers and glassware were removed and cleaned, furniture was French polished and the livery of participants was reworked where necessary. A new red carpet was ordered, but because the pile was very thick the Queen ordered it to be cut down slightly to make it easier for people wearing long robes to walk with ease. A temporary annexe was erected to include a royal robing room and a place for marshalling the processions. There was also a table, covered with gold damask, for the regalia.

The allocation of seats and the regulations about the clothes to be worn was the responsibility of the Duke of Norfolk. Because more seats than ever before were allocated to representatives from the Commonwealth, not all members of the peerage could be accommodated. A ballot was held for those peers who had no official duties.

Rehearsals went on for a long time before the event. The troops had to rehearse, as did the carriages and horses. The clergy taking part in the ceremony and the

ABOVE: The royal group in the throne room of Buckingham Palace in honour of the Coronation of Queen Elizabeth II; including the Duke of Edinburgh, Prince Charles, Princess Anne, the Queen Mother and Princess Margaret.

Queen herself all worked hard to ensure the day went well.

Street decorations were also planned well ahead. The streets through which the Coronation procession would pass were particularly colourful – Whitehall, Trafalgar Square, Pall Mall, St James's Street, Piccadilly and then Hyde Park, Marble Arch, Oxford Street, Regent Street, Piccadilly Circus, Haymarket, through Admiralty Arch and finally down The Mall to Buckingham Palace. The lights in The Mall were switched on by the Queen from Buckingham Palace. Immediately before the day windowboxes along the route were filled with fresh flowers – London was full of colour and beauty.

There was much speculation about the form the Queen's dress would take. Her wedding dress had been wonderful, but everyone expected her Coronation gown to surpass that. Norman Hartnell, who had designed the wedding dress, was asked to create the Coronation gown. The wonderfully colourful train, which is known as the robe, was embroidered by the Royal School of Needlework.

Although 2 June was not the beautifully sunny day that was hoped for, nothing could spoil the emotions and excitement of the coronation. On the following day the Queen and Prince Philip toured the East End and later that day the Queen presented medals to the armed forces and police from around the world who had

participated in the Coronation procession. London crowds were thrilled to see the Gurkha and Pakistani pipers coming from Buckingham Palace. On 9 June there was the Thanksgiving Service to mark the coronation at St Paul's Cathedral. All the royal family were there, and the lesson was read by Sir Winston Churchill.

On 4 and 5 June there were more tours to various parts of London, and Westminster Abbey was opened to the public for a month so that people could admire the wonderful setting. Later in the month the queen attended Derby, and everyone hoped her horse Aureole would be a winner. It came in second. Gordon Richards rode Pinza, the winning horse.

Beacons

From early times beacons have been lit throughout Britain. They would warn the population of a possible invasion, such as the approach of the Spanish Armada in the reign of Elizabeth I, and they were prepared in 1953 for the Coronation of the second Elizabeth. In the evening of 2 June 1953 they were lit, lighting up the sky, from the north to the south, from the east to the west, across Great Britain.

Events of 1953

ABOVE: The coffin of Soviet political leader Joseph Stalin (1879–1953) is carried from the House of Trade Unions, Moscow, Soviet Union.

January

There is alarm in Kenya at the growing threat posed by the Mau Mau, and 1,000 white settlers march to Government House to see Sir Evelyn Baring and demand more say in running the colony.

Josip Tito, whose name became known and admired in Britain for his resistance to the Germans in the war, becomes the president of Yugoslavia.

February

The east coast of England is devastated by floods caused by hurricanes and high tides as sea defences collapse from north Kent to Lincolnshire.

Holland suffers from flooding as the dykes burst.

The Federation of Rhodesia and Nyasaland joins the self-governing colony of Southern Rhodesia.

Twentieth Century Fox Film Corporation announces plans to convert its movie-making to wide screen Cinemascope.

Members of Parliament give a second reading to a private member's bill to simplify English spelling.

March

Joseph Stalin, who has ruled Russia for nearly 30 years, dies aged 73.

In East Germany 5,000 people seek asylum in the West.

Marshall Tito, president of Yugoslavia, visits Britain, the first communist head of state to visit Britain.

In New York the Swede Dag Hammarskjold is chosen as the Secretary General of the United Nations to succeed Trygve Lie.

April

In Kenya the army captures many members of Mau Mau.

It is reported in Britain that air travel over Easter was 20 per cent more than in 1952.

The budget cuts income tax by 6d (2½p) in the pound.

Sir Winston Churchill is invested as a Knight Companion of the Order of Garter.

Two Cambridge scientists, James D. Watson and Francis Crick, solve the mystery of DNA – the material of the genes – by which characteristics are passed from parent to offspring.

May

A cheering crowd greets 22 British prisoners-of-war on their return from Korea.

Arsenal win the Football League Championship for the seventh time.

King Hussein of Jordan and King Feisal II of Syria are crowned.

Chris Chataway sets a new record for 2 miles (3.2 km) of 8 mins 49.6 secs.

Edmund Hillary and the sherpa Tenzing Norgay reach the summit of Mount Everest.

June

Ethel and Julius Rosenberg are executed for revealing US atomic secrets to the Soviet Union.

Sir Winston Churchill is partly paralysed by a stroke.

CONSOMMÉ ST GEORGE

ST GEORGE CONSOMMÉ

Although the title of the soup could mean a chicken or other consommé named in honour of St George, patron saint of England, or St George's Chapel, Windsor, I have given the classic Consommé St George, often called Georges. This is made from a hare, which could have been caught on royal estates and been available at Buckingham Palace.

PREPARATION TIME: 1 HOUR, INCLUDING STOCK, CONSOMMÉ AND QUENELLES

COOKING TIME: 2 HOURS FOR STOCK, 15 MINUTES FOR CONSOMMÉ

   AND QUENELLES

SERVES: 6–8

Consommé

1 hare, skinned and jointed
2.5 litres (4 pints) water
2 onions
2 carrots
100 g (3½ oz) mushrooms
2 fresh bay leaves
1 sprig of tarragon
1 small bunch of parsley
300 ml (½ pint) claret
salt and pepper
sliced truffles, to garnish
Hare Quenelles (see right)

Cut away the flesh from the large legs and the saddle (back). Put this on one side. Put the leg and saddle bones into a large saucepan with the rest of the hare. Omit the liver and heart, which make an over-strong stock.

Add the water with the onions, carrots, mushrooms and herbs. Add a little salt and pepper. Weigh out 225 g (8 oz) of the reserved flesh for the hare quenelles.

Add the rest of the hare flesh to the pan and simmer for 2 hours. Strain the stock; there should be 1.5 litres (2½ pints) and any over should be used to poach the quenelles.

Remove a very little of the cooked hare from the mixture; this will be used as garnish. Heat the stock again for 10 minutes, then strain through muslin. For extra clarity it can be cleared with egg whites (see page 89).

While making the stock and consommé prepare the quenelles (see below). Heat the consommé with the claret. Garnish with tiny shreds of hare, shredded truffle and quenelles.

Hare Quenelles

225 g (8 oz) hare flesh, finely minced
½ teaspoon finely grated lemon rind
1 teaspoon chopped thyme
1 egg
2 tablespoons hare stock or claret
2 tablespoon very fine soft breadcrumbs
salt and pepper
1 egg white
hare stock (see left) or water (see method)

Pound the hare flesh to make it very smooth. Mix with the lemon rind and thyme. Separate the egg, stir the yolk into the hare mixture with the stock or claret, breadcrumbs and salt and pepper. Whisk the 2 egg whites, beat a tablespoon into the hare mixture then fold in the remaining whites.

Heat enough stock or seasoned water to give a depth of 5 cm (2 inches). Drop spoonfuls of the mixture into the liquid and cook for 4–5 minutes then lift out of the liquid and drain. The quenelles puff up during cooking. Add some to the soup just before serving. Serve any leftover separately.

Rosettes de Saumon Edinburgh

ROSETTES OF EDINBURGH SALMON

This salmon dish seems to be the same as that given on page 90. As there is no classic garnish 'Edinburgh', the name was undoubtedly given to the dish in honour of the Duke of Edinburgh.

FILET DE BOEUF POÊLE PALAIS

GRILLED FILLET STEAKS

The title means this dish would be made of prime British fillet steaks cooked on the stove at the palace. The fillets could be fried or grilled. There is no mention of a garnish or sauce so I have given maître d'hotel butter here, and there is a recipe for a classic accompaniment, béarnaise sauce, on page 149.

PREPARATION TIME: 15 MINUTES PLUS TIME FOR THE BUTTER TO CHILL

COOKING TIME: SEE METHOD

SERVES: 4

4 fillet steaks
50 g (2 oz) butter, melted
Maître d'hotel butter
50 g (2 oz) butter
1 tablespoon finely chopped parsley
2 teaspoons lemon juice
salt and pepper

Prepare the butter mixture well in advance so it has time to chill and harden. Cream the butter, add the rest of the ingredients and form into a neat oblong shape about 1 cm (½ inch) thick. When it is firm, cut it into 4 neat shapes.

Lightly season the steaks with salt and pepper immediately before cooking. Early salting brings out the meat juices, which should be avoided. Brush the meat with some of the melted butter, place on the rack of a grill pan and cook under a preheated hot grill.

For lightly cooked (rare) steaks 2–2.5 cm (¾–1 inch) thick, allow 2½–3 minutes, turn the steaks over, brush with the remaining butter and cook for a further 2½–3 minutes.

For medium steaks, cook as above then lower the heat and allow a further 1–2 minutes on either side.

Serve the steaks topped with maître d'hotel butter, with peas, new potatoes and salade mimosa (see right).

Variation

The steaks can be fried in hot butter, or butter and oil. Allow the same cooking times as above.

SALADE MIMOSA

MIMOSA SALAD

There are three entirely different classic recipes for this salad; the first is below and the other two are described under Variations.

PREPARATION TIME: 10 MINUTES

COOKING TIME: 10 MINUTES TO COOK EGGS

SERVES: 4

1 large bunch of watercress
1 small round lettuce, quartered
Mayonnaise (see page 129)
yolks of 2 hard-boiled eggs

Arrange sprigs of watercress and lettuce quarters on a flat dish. Top with a little mayonnaise. Rub the egg yolks through a coarse sieve over the salad to give the effect of mimosa flowers.

Variations

Use a Vinaigrette Dressing (see page 34) instead of mayonnaise.

An entirely different Salade Mimosa is made by combining lettuce, orange segments, sliced bananas and deseeded grapes. This salad should be dressed with lemon-flavoured double cream.

A third version of the salad is made by mixing pea-shaped rounds of truffles, balls of cooked carrots, chopped celeriac and diced cooked potatoes. Add a little mayonnaise and garnish with asparagus tips.

Whip the egg whites until stiff, beat 1 tablespoon of the whites into the raspberry mixture then fold in the remainder. Spoon into the prepared soufflé dishes and freeze. To serve, carefully ease away the paper surrounds on the soufflé dishes.

Always allow the dishes to stand in the refrigerator for 15 minutes before serving, so the mixture softens slightly and is not too hard. Top with the raspberries and a dusting of icing sugar.

Asperges with Sauce Mousseline

See the recipe on page 94.

SOUFFLÉS GLACÉS PRINCESSE ANNE

ICED SOUFFLÉ PRINCESS ANNE

Iced soufflés look impressive and are easy to prepare. This recipe is named after the young Princess Anne, but it does contain a little alcohol, and it is not a dish for children but for adults. The dish can be made without alcohol.

PREPARATION TIME: 20 MINUTES PLUS TIME TO FREEZE THE SOUFFLÉS

COOKING TIME: 10 MINUTES

SERVES: 6–8

2 eggs

50 g (2 oz) caster sugar

150 ml (¼ pint) single cream

150 ml (¼ pint) raspberry purée

1 tablespoon kirsch

300 ml (½ pint) double cream

To decorate

175 g (6 oz) raspberries

25 g (1 oz) icing sugar, sifted

Separate the eggs and put the yolks, caster sugar and single cream into the top of a double saucepan or into a basin. Place over a pan of hot, but not boiling, water and whisk until thickened. Remove from the heat; cool then add the raspberry purée and liqueur. The mixture can be sieved or liquidized to ensure a very smooth mixture.

Whip the double cream until it stands in peaks and blend with the cold raspberry mixture. Pour into a container and freeze lightly until like thick cream.

Meanwhile, prepare 6–8 small soufflé dishes. Tie a strong band of lightly oiled or buttered greaseproof or baking paper around the dishes to stand 2.5–3.5 cm (1–½ inch) above the rims. This supports the soft mixture.

MIGNARDISES ASSORTIES

DOILY DISHES

This refers to a mixture of dainty dishes, such as those described on page 54.

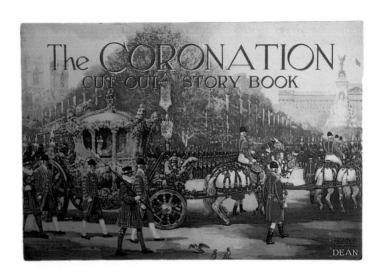

1953

CORONATION BUFFET

Throughout Britain people gathered to watch the Coronation of Elizabeth II on BBC Television. Although television had returned in 1946, after a break during the war years, only a few homes had sets, so anyone who owned one held 'open-house' for friends and neighbours.

By 1953 many foods were being derationed, and by June of that year only fats and meat were still controlled, so anyone planning special celebrations had to accept the fact that dishes based on those foods would have to be limited. However, during 1953 fresh eggs, cream and sweets (including chocolate) were freed from controls. There were plentiful supplies of fruit and vegetables, both home-grown and imported.

Although the television pictures were in black and white and the screens were fairly small, it was wonderful to watch the events as they happened. This is the menu I served on that day. The quantities here will serve 8 people, but I had well over twice that number, and because we were fairly crowded, I made everything easy to serve.

MENU

TO SERVE WITH DRINKS ON ARRIVAL
AVOCADO DIP WITH CRUDITÉS
CHEESE STRAWS AND CHEESE SOUFFLÉ TARTS
POTATO CRISPS
SALTED NUTS
MELON AND ORANGE COCKTAILS
SEAFOOD AND RICE RAMEKINS
CORONATION CHICKEN
DUCK AND APPLE SALAD
POTATO AND RUSSIAN SALADS
GOOSEBERRY FOULES
SUMMER MERINGUE NESTS
MIXED ICE CREAMS

DRINKS
SOFT DRINKS
SWEET AND DRY SHERRY
CHABLIS
CHÂTEAU MARGAUX
CHAMPAGNE

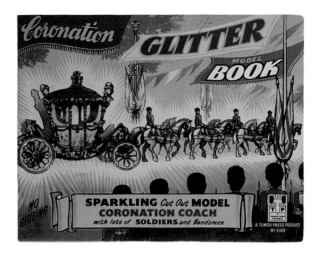

AVOCADO DIP WITH CRUDITÉS

If you are entertaining a large number of people, it is sensible to prepare several large platters or small trays of the crudités with small bowls of dip in the middle.

Avocados were still relatively new to people in 1953, and I chose them to form the basis of the dip, as I thought they would be a good talking point while we waited for the Queen to arrive at Westminster Abbey.

PREPARATION TIME: 25 MINUTES

SERVES: 8

2 tablespoons lemon juice, or to taste

2 large or 3 small ripe avocados

3 tablespoons Mayonnaise (see right) or Salad Cream (see page 61)

2 tablespoons finely snipped chives

4 tablespoons double cream, unwhipped

salt and pepper

Crudités

small sticks of raw carrots, celery heart, cucumber (peeled), red and green peppers, radishes (with a little stalk)

Prepare the lemon juice before cutting the avocados. Put the juice into a bowl. Halve the avocados, remove the stones and then the skin. Mash the pulp with the lemon juice then add the remaining ingredients. Taste and add more lemon juice if required.

Variation

When yogurt became available, it was often used instead of cream, giving a lighter mixture.

Mayonnaise

One of the surprising aspects of the 1950s was that olive oil and corn oil were both being used more often. It was now possible to buy olive oil in a grocer's shop or supermarket; previously, it was sold only by chemists.

Fresh eggs were available, which meant that mayonnaise could be made at home.

PREPARATION TIME: 15 MINUTES

SERVES: 8

2 yolks from large eggs

salt and pepper

up to 300 ml (½ pint) olive oil (but see Variations)

½ teaspoon made mustard, or to taste

½–1 teaspoon caster sugar, or to taste

up to 2 tablespoons lemon juice or vinegar (see Variations)

1 tablespoon boiling water, optional

Make quite sure the basin you are using is dry and free from any specks of grease. Bring the eggs out of the refrigerator early so that they and the oil are both at room temperature.

Put the egg yolks into a bowl with a pinch of salt and shake of pepper, the mustard and sugar. Beat or whisk, then very gradually beat in the oil drop by drop. When the sauce starts to thicken the oil can be added a little more rapidly.

The more oil that is used the thicker and richer the sauce becomes. Gradually add the lemon juice or vinegar, and finally add the boiling water, which makes the mayonnaise lighter.

Variations

In the 1950s there was little choice of olive oil, but now it is usual to choose extra virgin olive oil for mayonnaise, and to use other oils, or to use half olive oil and half another oil to give a lighter taste.

Wine vinegar was known in the 1950s, but it is now possible to use herb-flavoured vinegar or even a very little balsamic vinegar.

It is possible to make mayonnaise in a liquidizer or food processor (the former was available in 1953). Follow the procedure above but always add the oil slowly, with the machine in operation.

CHEESE STRAWS

Cheese was still rather scarce and it was necessary to accept whatever kind was in stock. This is the recipe I used.

PREPARATION TIME: 25 MINUTES

COOKING TIME: 7–10 MINUTES

MAKES: ABOUT 48

115 g (4 oz) plain flour

salt and cayenne pepper

½–1 teaspoon English mustard powder

115 g (4 oz) butter

85 g (3 oz) cheese, preferably Parmesan, very finely grated

1 egg yolk

To glaze

1 egg or 2 egg whites

2 teaspoons water

Sift the flour, salt, cayenne and mustard powder, rub in the butter, add the cheese and the egg yolk. Mix thoroughly then gather the mixture together. If the cheese is dry and the egg yolk small you may need a few drops of water to bind the mixture. Roll out the dough on a lightly floured surface until it is 5 mm (¼ inch) thick. Cut into fingers about 5 mm (¼ inch) wide and 7.5 cm (3 inch) long. Place them on lightly greased baking sheets. Whisk the egg or egg whites with a few drops of water. Brush over the biscuits.

   Bake in a preheated oven, 220°C (425°F), Gas Mark 7, for 7–10 minutes until pale golden in colour. Cool on the baking sheets for 5 minutes then lift on to wire racks. When cold store in an airtight tin.

CHEESE SOUFFLÉ TARTS

You can prepare the pastry and the simple filling ingredients then put the two together and bake the tarts just before serving. Make sure the pastry is very thin. Although the tarts look more impressive when freshly cooked, because the filling rises up like a soufflé, they still taste good if served cold.

PREPARATION TIME: 20 MINUTES

COOKING TIME: 12–15 MINUTES

MAKES: ABOUT 18

Pastry

225 g (8 oz) plain flour

pinch of salt

115 g (4 oz) butter or margarine or use half lard and half butter or margarine

water to bind

Filling

3–4 level tablespoons tomato or other chutney

4 large eggs

salt and cayenne pepper

115 g (4 oz) mature Cheddar cheese, finely grated

2 tablespoons very finely chopped parsley

Make the pastry as described on page 68. Roll it out thinly and cut into rounds to fit 18 small patty tins. Put a scant teaspoon of chutney into each pastry case.

   Separate the eggs and beat the yolks with the salt, cayenne, cheese and parsley. Whisk the whites until they stand in soft peaks. Take 2 tablespoons egg white and beat into the egg yolk mixture. Fold in the remaining egg whites. Spoon into the pastry cases. Bake in a preheated oven, 220°C (425°F), Gas Mark 7, for 12–15 minutes. Serve hot if possible,

Variation

Add 1 tablespoon sesame seeds to the cheese filling.

Melon and Orange Cocktails

This is the kind of hors d'oeuvre that both children and adults enjoy.

PREPARATION TIME: 15 MINUTES

SERVES: 8

4 large oranges

2 medium melons

sugar if required

mint leaves

Cut away the skin and pith from the oranges, working over a basin so that no juice is wasted. Next cut out the orange segments, discarding the skin and pips. Cut each orange segment into halves or quarters.

Halve the melons and remove the seeds. Scoop out the pulp with a vegetable baller. Mix the orange segments and melon balls. Spoon into sundae glasses with enough orange juice to moisten. Sweeten if desired. Chill well and top with mint leaves.

SEAFOOD AND RICE RAMEKINS

This combination of ingredients makes an excellent starter. It can be prepared in advance and heated through if you plan to serve it hot. In 1953 frozen peeled prawns were not available: prawns were fresh and had to be peeled. The weight given here is for peeled prawns.

PREPARATION TIME: 25 MINUTES

COOKING TIME: 20 MINUTES

SERVES: 8

50 g (2 oz) long grain rice

3 tablespoons Mayonnaise (see page 129)

3 tablespoons single cream

150 g (5 oz) cooked crabmeat

150 g (5 oz) cooked or canned salmon, flaked

150 g (5 oz) prawns, weight when peeled, chopped

2 tablespoons diced gherkins

1 tablespoon chopped capers

1 tablespoon lemon juice

2 tablespoons finely chopped parsley

salt and pepper

Topping

50 g (2 oz) butter

50 g (2 oz) soft coarse breadcrumbs

To garnish

8 lemon wedges

Cook the rice in salted water, as directed on the packet. If any moisture remains, strain well. Mix the hot rice with the mayonnaise and cream and allow to cool. Mix in all the fish, the gherkins, capers, lemon juice and parsley. Season to taste with salt and pepper.

Heat the butter in a frying pan; do not allow it to get too brown. Add the crumbs and turn these in the hot butter. If you are serving the ramekins hot, do not crisp the crumbs. Spoon the mixture into individual ovenproof ramekin dishes. Top with the crumbs, to cover the rice and fish mixture completely. Cook in a preheated oven, 200°C (400°F), Gas Mark 6, for 15–18 minutes.

If you are serving the ramekins cold, continue to heat the crumbs in the butter until they are crisp and golden brown. Remove from the pan and leave to cool. Fill the ramekins with the mixture. Cover with the cold, crisp crumbs.

Top hot or cold ramekins with the lemon wedges.

CORONATION CHICKEN

This was the dish of Coronation time, and it was extremely good. Chickens were easily obtainable by 1953, and they were well flavoured because they were free range. The following recipe gives 8 small portions and is a good partner to the Duck and Apple Salad.

PREPARATION TIME: 25 MINUTES

COOKING TIME: 1 ¼ HOURS

SERVES: 8

Cooking the chicken
1 chicken, about 2 kg (4 lb) when trussed
1 onion sliced
2–3 carrots, sliced
small sprig of parsley
small sprig of tarragon
salt and pepper
Salad
300–375 g (10–12 oz) canned apricots in syrup
2 tablespoons apricot syrup from can
225 ml (7 ½ fl oz) Mayonnaise (see page 129)
2 teaspoons curry paste, or to taste
4 tablespoons single cream
85 g (3 oz) blanched flaked almonds
salad ingredients

Place the chicken in a large saucepan with the other ingredients for cooking. Cover with water and simmer gently until just tender. When cold, remove the skin, take the meat off the bones and cut into bite-sized pieces.

Drain the canned apricots, save 2 tablespoons of the syrup (the rest can be used in a fruit salad). Cut the apricots into thin slices. Mix the mayonnaise with the curry paste, cream and apricot syrup. Add the chicken, sliced apricots and half the nuts.

Pile neatly on to a dish and top with the remaining nuts. Serve in a border of finely shredded lettuce, sliced tomatoes and cucumber.

DUCK AND APPLE SALAD

In the early 1950s duck was not particularly popular because it was widely (and mostly correctly) believed that ducks were too fatty and greasy. As a family we have always enjoyed duck, and, even in the 1950s, if it was cooked correctly the excess fat ran out in cooking.

This salad blends well with Coronation Chicken, so offer 8 small portions.

PREPARATION TIME: 25 MINUTES

COOKING TIME: 1 ½ HOURS

SERVES: 8

1 duckling, about 2.25 kg (5 lb) when trussed
1 tablespoon clear honey
4 dessert apples, peeled and cored
1 celery heart, diced
¼ small cucumber, peeled and diced
4 medium tomatoes, skinned and neatly diced
Dressing
2 tablespoons olive oil
2 tablespoons cider vinegar
1–2 teaspoons Dijon mustard
salt and pepper
1–2 teaspoons honey, or to taste
To garnish
lettuce, shredded
watercress sprigs

Stand the duckling on a rack in a roasting tin. Place in a preheated oven, 200°C (400°F), Gas Mark 6, and cook for 30 minutes. Lightly prick the skin so that excess fat spurts out, then return to the oven and prick again after another 30 minutes cooking. At the end of 1 ¼ hours prick for the final time, brush the skin with the honey and return to the oven for the remaining 15 minutes. If the duck is becoming too brown towards the end of the cooking time reduce the heat slightly.

Allow the duck to become cold, remove the skin and cut into narrow strips. Cut the lean flesh into bite-sized pieces, discarding any surplus fat on the body.

Mix the duck meat, apples, celery, cucumber and tomatoes. Mix together the ingredients for the dressing and spoon over the duck mixture.

Arrange the lettuce and watercress on a dish or individual plates, top with duck salad and then pieces of crisp duck skin.

Variation

Choose extra virgin olive oil if possible.

Potato Salad and Russian Salads
See the recipes on page 70.

GOOSEBERRY FOULE

Gooseberries were plentiful at the time of the Coronation and are ideal for a fruit foule (or fool, as it tends to be called). Although I generally mash, rather than sieve, the fruit – as in the original recipe – this time I thought it would be easier to eat at a buffet if I made a smooth mixture. Use the larger amount of gooseberries given in the recipe to ensure 750 ml (1¼ pints) purée.

Another decision was not to use all cream in the dessert, which was my original intention. Like all keen cooks, I was delighted to have cream once more, after all the years of being without, but as I was using this in several recipes I elected to use custard plus a little cream so that I did not make an over-rich menu.

PREPARATION TIME: 20 MINUTES

COOKING TIME: 15 MINUTES

SERVES: 8

675 g–1 kg (1½–2 lb) gooseberries

3 tablespoons water

85 g (3 oz) caster sugar, or to taste

600 ml (1 pint) thick custard, made with custard powder

150 ml (¼ pint) double cream, whipped

To decorate

150 ml (¼ pint) double cream, whipped

angelica leaves

Top and tail the gooseberries and put them in a saucepan with the water. Cook slowly and watch carefully because this is relatively little water but you do need a stiff mixture. When nearly soft, stir in the sugar. Adding this later softens the gooseberry skins better. Sieve the fruit, or put it into the liquidizer (often called the blender in those days), to make a smooth purée. When cold, mix with the cold custard and the cream.

Spoon into small sundae glasses or dishes and chill well. Top with cream and angelica leaves.

Variations

For a smooth, velvety texture, liquidize the mixture of fruit and custard before adding the cream.

A rich foule is made by using all whipped cream with the fruit and no custard.

SUMMER MERINGUE NESTS

The de-control of fresh eggs in 1953 made a great difference to our cooking. Dried eggs had been a great help when the fresh egg ration was so low, but now we could produce meringues and really good soufflés. Electric mixers were becoming readily available, so whisking could be done easily.

PREPARATION TIME: 25 MINUTES

COOKING TIME: ABOUT 2 HOURS

MAKES: 8

Meringues

3 egg whites

few drops of vanilla extract (see page 37)

175 g (6 oz) caster sugar

Filling

4 tablespoons lemon curd

4 tablespoons whipped cream

8 small firm strawberries

about 225 g (8 oz) raspberries

few redcurrants

To glaze

2 tablespoons redcurrant jelly

2 teaspoons water

Check the bowl is dry and free from grease. Whisk the egg whites with the vanilla until soft; do not over-whip them. Gradually whisk in the sugar or whisk in half the amount and fold in the remainder. Cover 1 or 2 baking sheets with baking paper or brush with a little oil.

Fit a 5 mm (¼ inch) plain or rose nozzle into a large piping bag and spoon in the mixture. Pipe 8 small rounds on the baking sheets then pipe circles around these. Put the meringues in a preheated oven, 90–110°C (200–225°F), Gas Mark ¼, and dry them out for 2 hours or until firm and crisp, then carefully remove from the baking sheets. When quite cold, the meringues can be stored in an airtight tin, away from any other foods.

Just before serving, mix the lemon curd and cream and spoon into each meringue case. Top with the fruit. Warm the redcurrant jelly with the water. Brush this glaze over the fruit.

Variation

In the 1950s we often used half caster and half sifted icing sugar instead of all caster sugar.

Mixed Ice Creams

Use double the quantities given in the recipe on page 95. Divide the mixture into 3 basins. Leave one batch as vanilla ice cream.

Chocolate Ice Cream

Blend 2 teaspoons cocoa powder or 4 teaspoons chocolate powder with 1 tablespoon hot water, cool and stir into the second batch of mixture.

Coconut Ice Cream

Stir 40 g (1½ oz) desiccated coconut into the remaining mixture with a very few drops green food colouring.

Variation

Rather than using desiccated coconut, shred or grate 50 g (2 oz) creamed coconut, dissolve in 1 tablespoon hot milk then cool and add to the basic mixture.

1953

A CORONATION STREET PARTY

Although the feelings of jubilation may have been very similar in 1977, there were great differences in the kind of food the people enjoyed at street parties in 1953 compared with that offered at Jubilee parties. In June 1953 rationing of fats and meat was still in force, but a wider range of foods, including citrus fruits, bananas, peaches and nuts, was plentiful, so we were able to enjoy a more varied diet than in the late 1930s.

BELOW: Residents in London enjoying themselves at a street party to celebrate Queen Elizabeth II's Coronation.

Sweets came off ration in February 1953, to the joy of children and adults alike. Fresh eggs were derationed in March 1953, so the dishes made for Coronation parties could be based on fresh, rather than dried, eggs.

We had been without fresh cream since 1940, but it became available again in April 1953, and this meant that many dishes were adorned with the real thing, rather than the mock creams we had become used to making for 13 long years. The chief difference, however, lies in the choice of foods in 1977 and in 1953. By the 1970s many children and adults had travelled abroad and had eaten in restaurants serving foreign foods in this country. This meant they had experienced a wide range of dishes from other countries which had been incorporated into our cuisine.

In 1953, on the other hand, our dishes were almost entirely based on traditional British fare, and we were still making the pre-war favourites we had been without for so long. We relished our home-made savouries, cakes and pastries, some of which are described on the pages that follow.

MENU

BACON, EGG AND CHICKEN PIE WITH MIXED SALAD

HOME-MADE SAUSAGES ON STICKS

MIXED SANDWICHES

CHEESE SCONES

BANANA TEABREAD

ORANGE CAKE

COCONUT PYRAMIDS

CHOCOLATE JUMBLES

FRUIT JELLIES

ICE CREAM

TEA, ORANGE JUICE

BACON, EGG AND CHICKEN PIE

The dish incorporates three of the most popular foods of the day. Bacon was still rationed and chickens were not over-plentiful but, for this special event, they would be used in this delicious savoury. In the 1950s all bacon was sold with rinds. The pie is not suitable for freezing.

PREPARATION TIME: 25 MINUTES

COOKING TIME: 30 MINUTES

SERVES: 6

225 g (8 oz) plain flour

pinch of salt

50 g (2 oz) lard

50 g (2 oz) margarine

cold water to bind

Filling

225 g (8 oz) streaky bacon rashers

2 medium tomatoes, sliced

225 g (8 oz) cooked chicken, minced or finely chopped

1 tablespoon chopped parsley

4 eggs

salt and pepper

milk, to glaze

Sift the flour and salt into a mixing bowl, rub in the lard and margarine until the mixture looks like fine breadcrumbs. Gradually add enough cold water to bind. Wrap and chill for about 30 minutes if time permits. Roll out just over half the pastry and line an 18–20 cm (7–8 inch) round sandwich tin.

Remove the rinds from the bacon rashers; heat the rinds in a frying pan, to give some fat, then remove. Fry the bacon rashers, remove from the pan and chop finely.

Cook the sliced tomatoes in any fat remaining in the pan, add to the bacon rashers with the chicken and parsley. Spread this mixture over the pastry. Beat the 4 eggs, season lightly with salt and pepper then pour over the chicken layer. Moisten the edges of the pastry base. Roll out the remaining pastry and place over the filling; do not press this down too firmly. Seal the edges, make a slit in the centre of the pastry lid and

use any pastry left to make leaves to decorate the top of the pie. Brush with a little milk and bake in a preheated oven, 190°C (375°F), Gas Mark 5, for 25 minutes. Check at the end of this time and, if the pastry is not sufficiently brown, cook for a further 5–10 minutes. The filling ingredients will be adequately heated. Cut into slices and serve hot or cold with a mixed salad.

Salads

In the 1950s, salads generally consisted of a mixture of lettuce, sliced cucumber, sliced tomatoes, radishes and sliced hard-boiled eggs and were usually served with salad cream.

HOME-MADE SAUSAGES

Fresh meat was scarce and severely rationed, so butchers' sausages continued to lack both meat and flavour. People longed for a good sausage and would sometimes use part of their meat ration to make really meaty sausages.

A hand-mincer was used in many homes, but most butchers were obliging and would mince meat for their customers, and for a special occasion, such as a Coronation party, they would also often supply sausage casings.

PREPARATION TIME: 20 MINUTES

COOKING TIME: SEE METHOD

MAKES: 10 LARGE OR UP TO 30 BITE-SIZED SAUSAGES

450 g (1 lb) lean pork

3 fat bacon rashers, rinds removed

50 g (2 oz) soft breadcrumbs

1 tablespoon hot milk

1 tablespoon finely snipped chives

1 teaspoon finely chopped sage leaves or ½ teaspoon dried sage

pinch of allspice

salt and pepper

prepared sausage casings, to coat

Put the pork and bacon rashers through a mincer twice so that the meat is very fine. Soak the breadcrumbs in the hot milk, then mix them with all the other ingredients. Stir vigorously to give a mixture that will not disintegrate.

Put the mixture into a large piping bag with a plain nozzle and force the mix into the casing. Tie it at the required intervals.

Either fry the sausages in a very little hot fat for 8–10 minutes, depending on the size, or grill for the same time. If it is more convenient, bake the sausages in a preheated oven, 200°C (400°F), Gas Mark 6, for 15–25 minutes.

Variation

The sausages can be cooked without the casing, but they tend to break up when put on wooden cocktail sticks. If you prefer, use the sausagemeat in Sausage Rolls (see page 147) or on fingers of bread and butter.

Mixed Sandwiches

Although these sandwiches were for a party it is doubtful whether everyone would remove the crusts from the bread, for we still felt that no food should be wasted, but they would be cut into small, neat shapes. The sandwiches were mostly made with white bread, for after years of heavy national wholemeal bread and flour we thankfully returned to lighter white bread and flour.

The most usual fillings would be those based on eggs and potted meats and fish, for these were plentiful and children liked them. Some people enjoyed Marmite sandwiches, others disliked them intensely, but they were a feature of the 1950s.

Cheese was still rationed, but one of the popular and healthy sandwich fillings of the time was made by mixing equal amounts of finely grated Cheddar cheese and grated raw carrots with enough salad dressing to moisten the mixture. Salad dressing was more usual than mayonnaise.

Chopped cooked ham would be mixed with salad ingredients and salad dressing to make it go further, and small amounts of very finely chopped chicken would also be added.

There might well also be sweet sandwiches. The favourite fillings being mashed bananas, honey and jam.

CHEESE SCONES

Cheese, like all fats, was still rationed in 1953, but a relatively small amount of Cheddar cheese gives a good flavour to scones. Children generally like these, particularly when they are made quite small and topped with a little more cheese.

PREPARATION TIME: 15 MINUTES

COOKING TIME: 10–12 MINUTES

MAKES: 12 WHOLE SCONES OR 24 WHEN SERVED HALVED

225 g (8 oz) self-raising flour, or plain flour with 2 teaspoons baking powder, or ½ level teaspoon bicarbonate of soda and 1 level teaspoon cream of tartar
pinch of salt
shake of black pepper
pinch of mustard powder
25 g (1 oz) margarine
50 g (2 oz) strongly flavoured Cheddar cheese, finely grated
about 150 ml (¼ pint) milk

Sift the flour, or flour and baking powder or bicarbonate of soda and cream of tartar, with the salt, pepper and mustard powder. Rub in the margarine, add the cheese and enough milk to give a soft rolling consistency.

Roll out on a lightly floured board until nearly 2 cm (¾ inch) thick and cut into 12 rounds. Put on a lightly greased baking sheet and bake in a preheated oven, 220°C (425°F), Gas Mark 7, for 10–12 minutes or until firm when pressed at the sides.

Lift on to a wire rack and cover with a cloth if you want to keep the scones soft. Do not do this if you like them crisp on the outside.

To serve, halve and spread with butter then put the halves together again or spread with butter then top with grated cheese and/or small pieces of tomato or cucumber.

Variations

For a richer scone, mix with 1 beaten egg or egg yolk and milk

To give an attractive glaze on top, brush with beaten egg or milk before baking.

BANANA TEABREAD

Bananas were already becoming established as one of Britain's favourite fruits, and this teabread has an excellent flavour. It is best when freshly made, but it does freeze well.

PREPARATION TIME: 20 MINUTES

COOKING TIME: 1 HOUR

MAKES: 1 x 1 KG (2 LB) LOAF

2 large bananas
1 tablespoon lemon juice
50 g (2 oz) margarine
50 g (2 oz) caster sugar
2 eggs, beaten
225 g (8 oz) self-raising flour
50 g (2 oz) sultanas
50 g (2 oz) mixed candied peel, chopped
50 g (2 oz) halved walnuts, chopped
150 ml (¼ pint) milk

Grease and flour a 1 kg (2 lb) loaf tin. Mash the bananas with the lemon juice; cream the margarine and sugar until soft and light. Beat in the mashed bananas, then add the eggs, the sifted flour and the remainder of the ingredients. Spoon into the tin and bake in a preheated oven, 180°C (350°F), Gas Mark 4, for 1 hour or until firm to the touch.

Cool in the tin for 10 minutes, then turn on to a wire rack. Serve thinly sliced and spread with butter or margarine.

ORANGE CAKE

Although sugar and other sweetenings, such as golden syrup and preserves, were plentiful, fat was still rationed, so cakes tended to be made with generous amounts of sweetening and an economical quantity of fat. Make sure you use just the zest from the orange rind so the cake is not bitter. This cake freezes well.

PREPARATION TIME: 30 MINUTES

COOKING TIME: 55–60 MINUTES

SERVES: 8

115 g (4 oz) golden syrup

50 g (2 oz) marmalade, jellied type if possible

115 g (4 oz) butter or margarine

150 g (5 oz) caster sugar

2 teaspoons finely grated orange rind

175 g (6 oz) self-raising flour

50 g (2 oz) ground almonds

2 small eggs

3 tablespoons orange juice

To decorate

3 tablespoons marmalade

50 g (2 oz) almonds, blanched and chopped

Line a 20 x 15 cm (8 x 6 inch) oblong tin with greased greaseproof paper or baking paper.

To measure the golden syrup and marmalade, weigh the empty saucepan, then gradually spoon in the syrup and marmalade, checking the weight as you do so. Add the butter or margarine, caster sugar and orange rind. Stir over a low heat until the ingredients have melted, then leave until cool. Do not wash the saucepan.

Sift the flour with the ground almonds, add the syrup mixture and beat well. Whisk the eggs and stir into the mixture. Pour the orange juice into the saucepan, warm this and stir briskly, so it absorbs any ingredients left in the saucepan. Beat into the mixture then spoon into the tin. Place in a preheated oven, 150°C (300°F), Gas Mark 2, and bake for 55–60 minutes or until firm to a gentle touch.

Cool for 10 minutes in the tin then place on a wire rack. When cold remove the paper. Warm the marmalade and spread evenly over the top of the cake then top with the almonds.

Variation

This cake can be soaked in orange syrup. Put 1 tablespoon marmalade, 50 g (2 oz) caster sugar and 150 ml (¼ pint) orange juice into a saucepan, stir over the heat until the sugar melts then boil briskly for 3 minutes. Spoon the hot syrup over the cake as soon as it comes from the oven. Leave in the cake tin until cold. Cut into fingers and top with crystallized orange slices.

BELOW: Children eating the food on offer at a street party to celebrate the Coronation in London.

COCONUT PYRAMIDS

There are two ways of making these small cakes, and I have included both methods. Sweetened condensed milk was a favourite with many people, and children would doubtless prefer the slightly sticky texture that this gave to the pyramids. Adults, on the other hand, would like the crisper texture when they were made with egg whites. They freeze reasonably well, although they tend to become slightly crumbly.

By the early 1950s desiccated coconut was now available in Britain, but rice paper was less easy to obtain.

PREPARATION TIME: 10 MINUTES

COOKING TIME: 10 MINUTES

MAKES: 18

2 egg whites
175 g (6 oz) desiccated coconut
115 g (4 oz) caster sugar
2 teaspoons cornflour
rice paper

Whisk the egg whites until just frothy, add the rest of the ingredients. Form into small pyramid shapes with damp fingers. Place rice paper on baking sheets or grease these lightly or cover with baking paper.

Put the pyramids on the rice paper and bake in a preheated oven, 160°C (325°F), Gas Mark 3, for 10 minutes or until firm with golden brown tips. Cool slightly then lift off the baking sheets on to a wire rack. Cut away any surplus rice paper, if using this.

Alternatively, mix a 425 ml (15 fl oz) can of sweetened condensed milk with about 225 g (8 oz) desiccated coconut or sufficient to give a texture that can be formed into pyramids. Continue as above.

Variation

In either recipe the mixture can be tinted with a few drops of food colouring.

CHOCOLATE JUMBLES

The fact that chocolate was now unrationed meant that it could be used for cakes and desserts. These uncooked cakes had already become a great favourite. It is essential that the cornflakes are very crisp and the melted chocolate cool, although still soft enough to bind with the cereal. Plain chocolate is easier to melt than milk chocolate, take care it does not become overheated.

PREPARATION TIME: 10 MINUTES

COOKING TIME: FEW MINUTES TO MELT CHOCOLATE

MAKES: 10–12

150 g (5 oz) plain chocolate
50 g (2 oz) cornflakes

Break the chocolate into pieces, put into a large basin and melt over hot, but not boiling, water. Cool, then add the cornflakes and mix together. Do not be vigorous for this would break the cornflakes into too small pieces.

Spoon into small paper cases – these had become available again after years of paper shortage – and leave until set. If you have no paper cases, place each jumble on a lightly buttered baking sheet or dish. Leave until set then store in a cool place until ready to serve.

ICE CREAMS

Most homes were still without a refrigerator, so that only a small proportion of people could make ice cream at home. Those who owned a refrigerator were anxious to show what could be done, so would make ices. It was in about 1953 that I demonstrated the first home-made ice creams on television. I made several versions. The first was based on canned evaporated milk, which was used widely during the 1950s (see below) and considered an ideal choice for children as it was not too rich. The others were based on cream (see pages 37 and 94).

Vanilla Ice Cream

PREPARATION TIME: 20 MINUTES PLUS OVERNIGHT CHILLING

FREEZING TIME: 1–1½ HOURS

SERVES: 6

425 ml (15 fl oz) can unsweetened full cream evaporated milk
40–50 g (1½–2 oz) caster or icing sugar, sifted
about ½ teaspoon vanilla extract, or to taste

Chill the evaporated milk overnight in the refrigerator, which makes it easier to whip. Open the can and pour the milk into a large bowl, whisk until light and fluffy then fold in the sugar and vanilla. Pour into a freezing tray and freeze until firm.

Variations

The mixture could be flavoured with 1 tablespoon sifted cocoa or 2 tablespoons chocolate powder or 1–2 teaspoons liquid coffee essence, such as Camp.

For a fruit flavour, fold in 150 ml (¼ pint) thick, smooth fruit purée. Raw raspberries and strawberries should be sieved to remove all pips.

Note: At the time it was advised that the cold control on the refrigerator should be turned to the coldest setting 1 hour before making the ice cream. When it was frozen, the control was returned to the normal position.

Fruit Jellies

During the war years commercial jellies were scarce and had a very poor flavour. By 1953 jellies had returned to their prewar quality, and they were immensely popular. For special occasions, such as parties, the liquid jelly would be mixed with sliced canned or fresh fruits – sliced peaches or sliced fresh bananas – so it became much more interesting. To please children there would be colourful layers of different flavoured jellies spooned into individual dishes.

BELOW: Queen Elizabeth II greeting the public after a service at St Paul's Cathedral.

Silver Jubilee

1977

ABOVE: Three children dressed up in patriotic clothing to celebrate Queen Elizabeth II's Silver Jubilee.

MOST OF 1977 WAS DEVOTED TO THE CELEBRATIONS MARKING THE SILVER JUBILEE OF QUEEN ELIZABETH'S ACCESSION. DURING THAT YEAR QUEEN ELIZABETH AND PRINCE PHILIP UNDERTOOK VISITS TO THE COMMONWEALTH AND THROUGHOUT BRITAIN. IN FEBRUARY, THEY LEFT BRITAIN FOR AN EXTENSIVE TOUR, VISITING FIJI AND TONGA EN ROUTE FOR NEW ZEALAND AND AUSTRALIA. THE ROYAL COUPLE TRAVELLED EXTENSIVELY, WALKING AS MUCH AS POSSIBLE TO MEET THE PEOPLE. IN OCTOBER THE QUEEN OPENED THE CANADIAN PARLIAMENT BEFORE GOING TO THE BAHAMAS. SHE ALSO REVIEWED HER TROOPS IN WEST GERMANY.

In addition to overseas travel, the Queen visited as many places as possible in Britain, and it was estimated that during Jubilee year she travelled a total of 11,265 km (7,000 miles) in Britain and 59,580 km (37,000 miles) on her overseas visits.

Tuesday, 7 June was the day of the service at St Paul's Cathedral. The Queen and Prince Philip travelled from Buckingham Palace in the same golden state coach that had been used for the Coronation in 1953. Troops lined the route and about a million spectators crammed into the streets to cheer the royal couple. The service was attended by all the members of the royal family, by representatives of the Commonwealth and by distinguished people from many other countries.

After the service the Queen and Prince Philip walked to the Guildhall for the official luncheon so that the crowds could greet her. She accepted bouquets from people and shook their hands. Banners and placards proclaimed 'God Save our Queen' but perhaps the most impressive – which summed up the relaxed feeling – was 'Liz Reigns – OK!'. The Jubilee was a wonderful opportunity for people throughout Britain to celebrate with street parties and special events.

As well as celebrations throughout Jubilee year, Prince Charles organized the Silver Jubilee Appeal. The object was to raise money so that young people could help others. The appeal raised a total of £16 million.

Before the celebrations began, beacons and bonfires were prepared throughout Britain, and the Queen herself set light to the huge bonfire near Windsor Castle as the public prepared to celebrate the 25 years that had elapsed since she became Queen. The British economy was in very poor shape in 1977: unemployment was rising and inflation was rife. The Times pointed out that £1.00 had only the quarter of the value it had when the Queen ascended the throne in 1952, but it may have been because of the economic gloom that everyone welcomed the Silver Jubilee as a wonderful opportunity to forget their cares and enjoy the celebrations and show their affection for the Queen and the royal family.

Preparations had gone on during 1977 – souvenir mugs and many other

ABOVE: Queen Elizabeth II greeting the crowds at the celebration of her Silver Jubilee.

mementoes were produced – and towns and villages throughout Britain worked to make sure that their street parties were as exciting and colourful as possible. By June 1977 a much wider selection of foods was available than there had been in 1953. Holidays in Europe and further afield and more adventurous supermarkets and delicatessens had encouraged the British public to develop their taste for a more varied selection of dishes and ingredients. This meant there was not one general form of celebration, but a variety of different kinds.

There were celebrations in schools and in the streets. Younger children enjoyed food that was not greatly unlike earlier parties, but older children were now more interested in savoury dishes. Adults were proud to serve traditional British dishes at simple celebration suppers, and in spite of Britain's fickle weather, a growing number of people enjoyed an outdoor barbecue meal on that lovely sunny June day.

Events

of

1977

ABOVE: British jockey Tommy Stack on Red Rum is led in at Aintree after winning the Grand National, making Red Rum the first horse to win three Nationals.

January

In Salisbury, Rhodesia, Ian Smith rejects the peace proposals put by the British envoy.

The International Monetary Fund lends Britain £3.9 billion.

Roy Jenkins becomes the first president of the European Commission in Brussels.

Clive Sinclair introduces a 5 cm (2 inch) TV costing £175.00

Jimmy Carter is inaugurated as 39th president of the USA.

February

The government announces referendums about devolution of Scotland and Wales.

IRA terrorists are jailed for life for the Balcombe Street siege and murders.

The Space Shuttle makes its first test flight and lands safely.

The foreign secretary, Anthony Crosland, suffers a stroke and dies; he is succeeded by Dr David Owen.

In Uganda, Idi Amin forbids all UK residents to leave the country.

March

President Sadat of Egypt announces that he will not allow a single inch of Arab soil to remain under Israeli occupation.

In Britain, it is announced that prices have risen by 69.5 per cent since 1974.

The Labour Party (led by James Callaghan) and the Liberal Party (led by David Steele) agree a pact so that the Labour government will avoid defeat.

Two jumbo jets, belonging to KLM and Pan Am, collide on the ground in the Canary Islands; 582 people are killed.

April

Red Rum wins his third Grand National at Aintree, the first horse to achieve this.

British Aerospace is created to run Britain's nationalized aviation industry.

President Sadat of Egypt arrives in Washington to discuss the problems of peace in the Middle East.

In Brazil it is learned that Ronald Biggs – one of the train robbers, who escaped to South America – has attended a drinks party on a Royal Navy ship.

May

The Australian publisher, Kerry Packer, arranges for 35 of the world's best cricketers to play in a series of matches in Australia during the autumn.

Nigel Short, aged just 11 years old, qualifies as the youngest ever chess champion in a national contest.

Manchester United beats Liverpool in the FA Cup Final, but Liverpool wins the League Championship for a tenth time and beats the German champions to win the European Cup.

June

Lester Piggott has his eighth Derby win on The Minstrel.

Damage at Wembley is estimated at £15,000 when fans dig up the pitch after Scotland beats England 2–1.

Commonwealth leaders condemn Idi

Amin's violations of human rights. In Moscow, Leonid Brezhnev becomes head of state and secretary of the Communist Party.

July
In Washington the widow of murdered Martin Luther King is awarded the Medal of Freedom on her late husband's behalf.

Virginia Wade defeats Bette Stove of Holland to become the ladies' singles champion at Wimbledon; Bjorn Borg defeats Jimmy Connors to take the men's title.

The average price of a house in London and the southeast is now £16,731.

The licence fee for a colour TV is raised to £21.00; the licence for a black and white set becomes £9.00.

In Spain the first polling day for 41 years takes place after having been banned by General Franco but restored by King Juan Carlos.

August
Elvis Presley, the king of rock 'n' roll, dies at the age of 42.

In Salisbury, Rhodesia, a bomb in a Woolworth store kills 12 people.

New, smaller pound notes are introduced.

Geoffrey Boycott scores the hundredth century of his cricketing career at Headingley, Yorkshire.

September
Freddie Laker launches his first Skytrain plane service from Gatwick to New York as passengers queue for the walk-on flight that costs £59.00 (compared to the usual £186.00).

Maria Callas, the great opera singer, dies in her Paris flat at the age of 53.

Figures showed that for the first time motorists are buying more foreign cars than British ones.

October
The Nobel prize for peace is won by Betty Williams and Mairead Corrigan of the Northern Ireland Peace Movement.

Rudolf Nureyev stars as Rudolph in the ballet *Valentino*.

Bing Crosby dies of a heart attack at the age of 75 on a golf course near Madrid.

November
President Sadat of Egypt visits Israel, the first Arab leader to do so, having been invited to address the Knesset.

The United Nations place a mandatory and permanent ban on arms sales to South Africa.

December
Menachem Begin visits the USA and tells President Carter that Israel is ready to return the Sinai to Egypt.

The actor and director, Sir Charles Chaplin, dies at his home in Switzerland at the age of 88.

Amnesty International, the London-based organization, wins the Nobel peace prize for 'securing the ground for freedom'; Sir Nevill Mott is one of the winners of the physics prize for work on electronic solid-state circuitry.

ABOVE: An early promotional portrait of American rock n' roll singer and actor Elvis Presley, who died this year.

SILVER JUBILEE LUNCHEON

The luncheon served at the Guildhall in the City of London to celebrate the Queen's Silver Jubilee shows how meals in Britain had changed in the years since her Coronation. The menu is based mainly on British foods, but there are fewer courses than would have been served in earlier days. The choice of dessert is particularly interesting. In the past melon was considered ideal for a simple hors d'oeuvre, but in 1977 it was acceptable to offer it as part of a dessert.

BELOW: Queen Elizabeth II walking to the Guildhall in London for a city luncheon to celebrate the Silver Jubilee.

Luncheon in Celebration
of the Silver Jubilee of
Her Majesty
Queen ELIZABETH

◇

7 June 1977

MENU

◇

Hochheimer Konigin Victoria Berg
Salmon Trout Bellevue
Riesling 1975 (Deinhard)
Sauce Tarragon

◇

Gevrey-Chambertin 1971
Fillet of Angus Beef
(Calvet)
Béarnaise Sauce
New Buttered Potatoes
Broad Beans
Baby Carrots

◇

Château Climens 1969
Charentais Melon and Raspberries

◇

Dow's 1960
Coffee

SALMON TROUT BELLEVUE

This method of cooking and serving salmon trout is ideal for a summer's day. Although not particularly well known, the term Bellevue (often given as two words) gives a very attractive presentation. The trout are poached in court bouillon, and this liquid is then enhanced by other flavours and turned into a jelly to coat the fish. This gives it a moist texture.

Tarragon sauces are often based on cooked brown or white sauces, but these are unsuitable to serve with cold fish, so I have included a light mayonnaise-based version.

PREPARATION TIME: 35 MINUTES

COOKING TIME: COURT BOUILLON AND LIQUID FOR JELLY 35 MINUTES;
SALMON TROUT 8–10 MINUTES

SERVES: 4

4 small salmon trout

1 medium lobster, cooked

Tarragon Sauce (see page 144)

Court bouillon

450 ml (¾ pint) dry white wine

300 ml (½ pint) water

1 medium onion, sliced

1 medium carrot, sliced

1 sprig of parsley

1 small sprig of thyme

1 tablespoon olive oil

salt and pepper

Jelly

Court bouillon (as above)

lobster shells (see method)

1 tablespoon dry pale sherry

2 level teaspoons powder or 2 leaves gelatine

2 tablespoons white wine or water

1 tablespoon lemon juice, or to taste

To garnish

lobster shells

lemon wedges and sprigs of tarragon

lettuce

Split the salmon trout and remove the intestines. Scrape the fish and wash in cold water. Split the lobster, discard the spinal cord and crack the large claws. Remove the meat from the body and large claws but save the small claws for garnish. Wash and retain the body shells and those of the large claws.

Put the ingredients for the court bouillon into a fish kettle or large, shallow saucepan. Bring to the boil and simmer gently for 15 minutes, then strain. Return the liquid to the pan, add the salmon trout and simmer for 8–10 minutes or until just cooked but unbroken. Lift the fish out of the liquid. Drain well and keep cool. Strain the court bouillon again and pour into a smaller saucepan.

Add the lobster shells. Simmer for 10 minutes then add the sherry. Strain the liquid once more and measure it; you should have nearly 450 ml (¾ pint). Return this amount to the pan and heat. Soften the powder or leaf gelatine in the cold white wine; allow to stand for 3–4 minutes, then add to the hot liquid. Stir until dissolved and add lemon juice and salt and pepper to taste. Pour into a container and leave to cool until a syrupy consistency.

Skin the trout. The heads could be removed but that is a matter of personal preference. Arrange the fish on the serving dish with the lobster flesh neatly on or around the trout. Brush all the fish with the lightly set jelly and allow to set.

Whisk any jelly left and use as a garnish with the lobster, claws, lemon, tarragon and lettuce. Serve with tarragon sauce.

Tarragon Sauce

There are two types of tarragon, the wild variety, known as Russian tarragon, and the cultivated form, called French tarragon. The former is hardy and overwinters well, but the latter is delicate and has a much finer flavour. All tarragon has a strong flavour, so use it sparingly. The use of tarragon in the sauce to serve with the fish and also in béarnaise sauce was unusual – perhaps it was a favourite flavour of the Queen's.

PREPARATION TIME: 15 MINUTES

SERVES: 4

about 150 ml (¼ pint) Mayonnaise (see page 129)
1 tablespoon finely chopped tarragon, or to taste
1–2 tablespoons single cream

Make the mayonnaise as described. Add the chopped tarragon, then the cream.

Variations

A lighter sauce could be made by using half mayonnaise and half thick yogurt with the tarragon and cream.

Adding 1–2 teaspoons balsamic vinegar gives an interesting flavour and colour to the sauce.

FILLET OF ANGUS BEEF

The menu does not indicate whether the meat was cut into individual steaks or roasted as whole fillets (small joints). The timing for cooking individual steaks is given on page 126; if you are roasting the meat as a joint it should be carefully weighed and cooked in a preheated oven, 220°C (425°F), Gas Mark 7. Because fillet is extremely tender, do not overcook the meat; 10 minutes per 450 g (1 lb) and 10 minutes over should be ideal for rare beef. Fillet steak is also lean, so the meat should be coated with softened butter or olive oil before cooking to keep it moist.

Whether the Angus beef is served in fillets or carved for the guests, béarnaise sauce is an ideal accompaniment as are these vegetables.

New Potatoes

Never boil these too quickly, but let the water bubble gently. Strain when cooked but toss in plenty of melted butter and finely chopped parsley. In 1977, new potatoes always would be scraped before cooking.

Broad Beans

To enjoy these at their best, start the cooking early. Pod the beans and cook steadily. Do not add salt until towards the end of the cooking time, because early salting tends to make the beans tougher. When cooked, strain and cool sufficiently to handle. Carefully pull away and discard the skins around the individual beans. Reheat the tender beans in a little butter.

Baby Carrots

These are easily over-cooked and are much better if slightly crisp. Cook for 5 minutes in steadily boiling, lightly salted water, then test; they should be cooked.

BÉARNAISE SAUCE

This sauce is made in much the same way as Hollandaise sauce (see page 35), but it has a more piquant taste because of the flavouring of shallot, tarragon and other herbs.

PREPARATION TIME: 15 MINUTES PLUS TIME FOR HERBS TO INFUSE

COOKING TIME: 2–3 MINUTES

SERVES: 4

3 tablespoons white wine vinegar

1 shallot, finely chopped

¾–1 tablespoon chopped tarragon

1 sprig of thyme

1 fresh bay leaf

115 g (4 oz) butter

2 egg yolks

pinch of cayenne pepper

salt and pepper

little extra chopped tarragon, to garnish

Put the vinegar, shallot and herbs into a saucepan, bring to the boil and simmer for 2–3 minutes until the vinegar is reduced to 1½ tablespoons. Allow to stand until cold. Strain the vinegar. Some people like to put the shallot back into the sauce.

Cut the butter into small pieces and leave at room temperature. Put the egg yolks with the cayene, salt and pepper and strained vinegar into the top of a double saucepan or a basin over hot, but not boiling, water. Whisk until thick, then gradually whisk in the butter. Taste and adjust the seasoning and amount of vinegar. Stir in the shallot (if retaining this) and the extra tarragon.

Variation

Up to 175 g (6 oz) butter can be used, but this would be unusual by 1977.

CHARENTAIS MELON AND RASPBERRIES

The combination of fruits is both colourful and refreshing, and there are several ways in which the dessert could be served. The melon could be cut in half, deseeded and filled with lightly sweetened raspberries. In the 1970s, melon was often moistened with a little port wine before serving or the raspberries might have been flavoured with kirsch. Alternatively, the melon could be skinned and neatly sliced. The slices could be arranged around a neat mound of raspberries, which could be topped with cream, or sugar and cream could be served separately.

Finally, the melon could be halved and deseeded. The flesh could then be cut into small balls with a melon baller. Arrange layers of melon balls and raspberries in sundae glasses. Moisten with lightly sweetened fruit syrup or kirsch or arrange the melon balls and raspberries on plates. Rub some raspberries through a sieve to make a purée, sweeten and flavour with a little kirsch or white wine and pour the sauce around the fruit.

1977

STREET AND SCHOOL PARTIES

Most schools held special Jubilee parties, and the dishes below would have been included in a party for younger children and older teenagers, who were beginning to prefer more savoury dishes to cakes. These are the most popular dishes of the 1970s, and recipes for those not given elsewhere follow.

MENU

SANDWICHES

SAUSAGES ON STICKS

SAUSAGE ROLLS

SCOTCH EGGS

QUICHE LORRAINE

PIZZAS

CHEESE SCONES

SWEET SCONES

CHERRY TARTS

CHOCOLATE CAKE

CHOCOLATE ECLAIRS

CHOCOLATE AND JAM SWISS ROLLS

MERINGUES

BRANDY SNAPS

ICE CREAM

SANDWICHES

The sandwiches on page 96 were still popular in 1977. Pâté was frequently used in sandwiches, and there is a recipe on page 57.

What would have been different in 1977 was the appearance of the sandwiches, which would be cut into fancy shapes, such as hearts and diamonds. Although white bread was far more popular, brown bread would be used, especially in ribbon sandwiches.

Ribbon Sandwiches

Cut an equal number of brown and white slices of bread and spread with butter or margarine. Spread a brown slice with the filling then cover with white bread. Cut into narrow fingers. Continue like this and arrange the sandwich fingers on plates so you have the striped effect of ribbons.

Bridge Rolls

Bridge rolls were widely used instead of slices of bread. Bakers of the time produced very small bridge rolls, which would be ideal for parties for very young children.

SAUSAGES ON STICKS

Adults and young people enjoyed sausages, and the easy way to eat these is on cocktail sticks. Butchers made small 'cocktail' sausages of high quality, so there was no need to make your own as had been necessary in 1953. Cocktail sticks should never be offered to young children; they should hold the sausages in their fingers.

Prick and fry the small sausages in a little hot fat – either lard or cooking fat – for 10–12 minutes. Allow 25 g (1 oz) fat to cook 450 g (1 lb) sausages. Turn the sausages over several times during cooking. Drain on kitchen paper then put on wooden or attractive plastic cocktail sticks.

The small sausages can be cooked without extra fat under a preheated grill for the same length of time or baked in a greased tin for 20–25 minutes in a preheated oven, 190–200°C (375–400°F), Gas Mark 5–6.

SAUSAGE ROLLS

Although many people use shortcrust pastry when making sausage rolls (see Variation), most cooks made the richer flaky pastry.

PREPARATION TIME: 45 MINUTES PLUS TIME TO STAND

COOKING TIME: SEE METHOD

MAKES: 12–36

Flaky pastry
225 g (8 oz) plain flour
pinch of salt
175g (6 oz) butter or half butter and half lard
about 4 tablespoons ice cold water
1 teaspoon lemon juice
Filling
450 g (1 lb) sausagemeat
To glaze
1–2 eggs, beaten

Sift the flour and salt into a basin. Divide the fat into 3 portions. Rub one-third into the flour as though making shortcrust pastry. Mix the water and lemon juice and use this to bind the pastry into an elastic and pliable dough, softer than shortcrust pastry. Turn out on to a lightly floured surface.

Roll out to an oblong shape. Cut the second third of the fat into small pieces and dot over the top two-thirds of the dough. Bring up the fatless section and fold over the dough; this should look like an opened envelope. Bring down the top one-third or the dough, so making a closed envelope. Turn the dough at right angles, so the open end of the dough is towards you. Seal this end and the other end by pressing down with the rolling pin then press at regular intervals to 'rib' the pastry. Roll out the dough to an oblong shape again.

Add the remainder of the fat over the dough, as above. When the dough has been rolled out finally, fold in three, wrap and chill before using.

To make the rolls, roll out the flaky pastry to 5 mm (¼ inch) thick, cut into long strips. Roll out the sausagemeat to give a roll just under half the width of the pastry. Lay the sausagemeat down the centre of the pastry strip. Moisten the edges of the pastry with water and fold to enclose the sausagemeat. Seal and flake the edges of the long pastry rolls, then cut into required lengths. Make 2 slits on top of each roll with a sharp knife or kitchen scissors. The ingredients make about 12 large sausage rolls or 36 cocktail size.

Bake in a preheated oven, 220°C (425°F), Gas Mark 7. Small rolls take about 15 minutes, larger ones 25–30 minutes. When baking large rolls, reduce the heat to 190°C (375°F), Gas Mark 5 after 15–20 minutes. Serve hot or cold, but freshly made.

Variation

Make shortcrust pastry with 300 g (10 oz) flour and 150 g (5 oz) fat as described on page 68. Use as the flaky pastry above but bake at 200°C (400°F), Gas Mark 6, allowing the timing as above.

SCOTCH EGGS

These were a favourite picnic savoury but were also frequently included in party menus and served with a salad. Various brands of cooking fat were still favourite ingredients at this period and were used instead of lard for frying.

PREPARATION TIME: 15 MINUTES

COOKING TIME: 10 MINUTES PLUS TIME FOR COOKING EGGS

SERVES: 4–8

4 eggs, hard-boiled

450 g (1 lb) sausagemeat

Coating

2 tablespoons flour

1 large or 2 small eggs, beaten

50 g (2 oz) fine crisp breadcrumbs

salt and pepper

Frying

deep lard or cooking fat

To garnish

mixed salad

Cool and shell the eggs. Divide the sausagemeat into 4 portions and flatten each one to a square on a lightly floured board. Place an egg in the centre of each portion of sausagemeat and roll this around the eggs. Make sure the eggs are completely covered; seal all the joins and roll into a good shape.

Dust with seasoned flour then coat in the beaten egg and finally in the crumbs.

Bring the lard or cooking fat up to 170°C (340°F). To test without a thermometer drop a cube of 24-hour bread into the fat. It should take 1 minute to turn golden brown.

Put the scotch eggs in the hot fat and fry steadily for 10 minutes. Turn them around several times so they brown evenly. Remove from the fat and drain on kitchen paper. Cool, then halve across the centre and serve on a bed of mixed salad (made as page 61).

Variation

Use an oil suitable for frying instead of the lard or cooking fat.

Quiche Lorraine

The recipe for Quiche Lorraine given in the 1937 Coronation banquet (see page 95) is an excellent classic one. The cream can be replaced by milk to make the filling less rich.

PIZZAS

These were still regarded as something of a novelty by most people, although young people were becoming very enthusiastic about them. The pizzas for special Jubilee celebrations would undoubtedly come from specialist restaurants. The days of frozen pizzas lay ahead, as did the desire to make the Italian savoury.

CHEESE SCONES

See the recipe on page 138.

SWEET SCONES

The cream teas of Devon and Cornwall had become well known in other parts of Britain, and one of the most popular sweet dishes at this time were scones topped with cream and home-made jam.

PREPARATION TIME: 15 MINUTES

COOKING TIME: 10–12 MINUTES

MAKES: 12 WHOLE SCONES OR 24 WHEN HALVED

225 g (8 oz) self-raising flour or plain flour with 2 teaspoons baking powder

pinch salt

40–50 g (1½–2 oz) butter or margarine

40–50 g (1½–2 oz) caster sugar

about 150 ml (¼ pint) milk

Sift the flour, or flour and baking powder, with the salt. Rub in the butter or margarine, add the sugar and enough milk to give a soft rolling consistency.

Roll out on a lightly floured board until 2–2.5 cm (¾–1 inch) thick and cut into 12 rounds. Put on an ungreased baking sheet and place in a preheated oven, 220°C (425°F), Gas Mark 7. Bake for 10–12 minutes or until firm when pressed at the side.

Lift on to a wire rack. The scones can be covered with a cloth if you want to keep them soft (see Cheese Scones, page 138). Serve hot or cold with butter or cream and jam.

Variations

Make cream and jam scones for a party. Cut the cold scones through the centre and top with whipped or clotted cream and jam.

To make fruit scones add 50–75 g (2–3 oz) sultanas or other dried fruit to the mixture.

Raising agents

By 1977 there was a difference in the raising agents used in scone-making. Self-raising flour would be chosen by most people or plain flour with baking powder but not bicarbonate of soda and cream of tartar.

CHERRY TARTS

These were a favourite feature of many parties in Jubilee year. Fresh British cherries were plentiful in the 1970s, as were excellent canned cherries.

PREPARATION TIME: 30 MINUTES

COOKING TIME: 12–15 MINUTES

MAKES: 18

Sweet shortcrust pastry

225 g (8 oz) plain flour

140 g (4½ oz) butter or margarine

40 g (1½ oz) caster or sifted icing sugar

1 egg yolk

water to bind

Filling

300 ml (½ pint) water

50 g (2 oz) caster sugar

500 g (1 lb 2 oz) ripe cherries, stoned

2 tablespoons redcurrant jelly

1 level teaspoon arrowroot

Sift the flour into a mixing bowl, rub in the butter or margarine, and add the sugar, egg yolk and enough water to bind. Wrap and chill for a short time before rolling out on a lightly floured board. Cut into 18 rounds to fit small patty tins and bake blind for 12–15 minutes in a preheated oven, 190°C (375°F), Gas Mark 5.

To bake small tartlet cases blind, simply press down the pastry. You can prick it lightly but this is not essential. For larger tartlet or flan cases fill with greaseproof paper and baking beans or crusts.

When the pastry is cooked, lift the tartlet cases out of the tins, remove the greaseproof paper and beans and allow to cool.

Meanwhile, make the filling. Put the water and sugar into a saucepan. Stir over the heat until the sugar has dissolved. Add the cherries, simmer gently for 5 minutes then strain the cherries; allow them to cool then spoon into the cases.

Boil the liquid in the saucepan until reduced to 150 ml (¼ pint). Blend this with the arrowroot, pour back into the saucepan, add the jelly and stir over a moderate heat until the jelly has dissolved and the syrup is clear. Cool, then brush the cherries with this slightly thickened syrup and leave to become quite cold.

Variation

If you are using canned cherries, drain the fruit (which is generally stoned). Use the syrup from the can for the glaze. In the 1970s fruit was not canned in natural juices.

CHOCOLATE CAKE

The interest in chocolate and its popularity has grown through the years, and cooks tend to use chocolate, rather than cocoa, to give flavour to special cakes. Chocolate containing up to 70 per cent cocoa solids is ideal for cooking. This cake can be frozen, even when it has been decorated.

PREPARATION TIME: 35 MINUTES

COOKING TIME: 1 HOUR

SERVES: 8–10

150 g (5 oz) plain chocolate

1½ tablespoons water

¼ teaspoon vanilla extract

150 g (5 oz) butter

150 g (5 oz) caster sugar

1 level tablespoon golden syrup

5 large eggs

150 g (5 oz) self-raising flour

Filling and topping

100 g (3½ oz) milk chocolate

50 g (2 oz) butter

100 g (3½ oz) icing sugar, sifted

3 tablespoons apricot jam, sieved

To decorate

25 g (1 oz) plain chocolate, coarsely grated

Line a 20 cm (8 inch) cake tin with baking paper. Break the plain chocolate in pieces, put it into a basin with the water and vanilla extract and melt over a pan of hot water. Cool slightly. Cream the butter, sugar and golden syrup until soft and light, add the chocolate and beat again.

Whisk the eggs and beat gradually into the creamed mixture. Fold in the flour. Spoon into the cake tin and bake in a preheated oven, 180°C (350°F), Gas Mark 4, for 1 hour or until firm to the touch. Cool in the tin for 10 minutes then turn on to a wire rack and leave until cold. Cut the cake into 2 layers.

Break the milk chocolate into pieces and melt them. Leave to cool slightly. Cream the butter and icing sugar and add the melted chocolate. Spread the bottom layer of the cake with half the apricot jam and about

one-third of the chocolate mixture. Sandwich the layers together, then spread the remainder of the jam and then some of the chocolate mixture over the top. Use the remainder of the mixture to pipe a border around the top of the cake. Finally, sprinkle the top with the grated plain chocolate.

Chocolate Eclairs

See the recipe on page 98.

Ice Creams

By 1977 the selection of commercially made ice creams had grown, and many people would buy ice cream rather than make it at home. However, there are recipes on pages 94 and 137.

CHOCOLATE AND JAM SWISS ROLLS

This light sponge is a favourite with most people, especially when it is filled with rum- or brandy-flavoured cream. If you are making this for children, Vanilla Butter Icing (see right) would be more appropriate. The sponge and filling freeze well.

The air incorporated into the sponge by whisking means it is not essential to use self-raising flour nor to add baking powder to plain flour.

PREPARATION TIME: 20 MINUTES

COOKING TIME: 12 MINUTES

SERVES: 8

65 g (2½ oz) flour

15 g (½ oz) cocoa powder

3 large eggs

150 g (5 oz) caster sugar

1 tablespoon hot water

25 g (1 oz) butter, melted (optional)

Filling

225 ml (7 ½ fl oz) double cream

25 g (1 oz) caster sugar

1–2 tablespoons rum or brandy

It is essential to bake this sponge as soon as it is mixed, so it is important to heat the oven in plenty of time. Line a 30 x 23 cm (12 x 9 inch) tin with greaseproof paper or nonstick baking paper.

Sift the flour with the cocoa. Do this in good time and leave on a plate in the warmth of the kitchen, which helps to lighten the flour.

Break the eggs into a mixing bowl, add 115 g (4 oz) of the sugar and whisk until thick; you should be able to see the trail of the whisk. Fold in the flour and cocoa, then the hot water. The melted butter can be added just before cooking, which helps to make a more moist sponge.

Spoon the mixture into the prepared tin and tilt this so all the corners are filled evenly. Bake in the preheated oven, 190°C (375°F), Gas Mark 5, for about 12 minutes or until firm to gentle pressure.

While the sponge is baking, sprinkle the remaining 25 g (1 oz) caster sugar over a sheet of greaseproof paper or baking paper. Turn the sponge on to this, pull away the lining paper, then gently roll the sponge with the new paper in between. Leave until cold.

Whip the cream, fold in the sugar and rum or brandy. Unroll the sponge, remove the paper and spread with the cream, then reroll.

Variations

Instead of cream, use Vanilla Butter Icing. Cream 50 g (2 oz) butter with a few drops of vanilla extract and 100 g (3½ oz) sifted icing sugar until soft and light. Add just a little single cream or milk to give a soft spreading consistency.

For Jam Swiss Roll, follow the recipe but use 85 g (3 oz) flour and omit the cocoa. Turn out, remove the lining paper and spread with 6 tablespoons of warm (not hot) jam. Roll firmly. If necessary top with more caster sugar.

MERINGUES

Follow the instructions for making the meringue under Summer Meringue Nests on page 134, but pipe or spoon the mixture into rounds on the prepared baking sheets.

The quantities given on page 134 would make 12–16 good-sized meringues, which would be baked as the meringue nests, and about 40 very small meringues, which need about 1 hour at the oven settings given. Small children love these and they need not be sandwiched together with cream. Never sandwich meringues with whipped cream until just before serving.

BRANDY SNAPS

Follow the directions for making and baking the Brandy Snap Cups on page 94, but instead of pressing the cooked mixture around the base of small containers press them around the oiled handles of wooden spoons. When rolled and firm just slip the handles out of the crisp rolls.

Bibliography

Benton, William, *Encyclopaedia Britannica*, 1969

Chronicle of the 20th Century, Chronicle, 1988

Coronation Book of Queen Elizabeth II, Odhams Press Ltd., 1953

Davidson, Alan, *The Oxford Companion to Food*, Oxford University Press, 1999

Davies, Nicholas, *Elizabeth, Behind Palace Doors*, Mainstream Publishing Projects, 2000

Elizabeth Crowned Queen, Odhams Press Ltd., 1953

Escoffier, Auguste, *Ma Cuisine*, English language edition, Hamlyn, 1965

Golby, J.M., and Purdue, A.W., *King and Queens of Empire, British Monarchs 1760–2000*, Tempus Publishing Ltd. 1988

Hering's Dictionary of Classical and Modern Cookery, translated by Walter Bicket, Virtue & Company Ltd., 1977

Holden, Anthony, *The Queen Mother*, Sphere Books Ltd., 1985

James, Robert Rhodes, *A Spirit Undaunted. The Political Role of George VI*, Abacus, 1999

Junor, Penny, *Elizabeth II*, Conran, 1991

Moynaham, Brian, *The British Century*, Weidenfeld & Nicolson Ltd., 1997

New Larousse Gastronomique, Hamlyn, 1960

Plumptre, George, *Edward VII*, Pavillion Books Ltd., 1995

Rose, Kenneth, *King George V*, Phoenix Press, 1983

Senn, G. H. *The Menu Book*, Ward, Lock & Co. Ltd., 12th edition

Yesterday's Britain, Reader's Digest Association Ltd., 1998

Index

Acknowledgements

The Coronation Menus:

Hamlyn and Marguerite Patten would acknowledge with grateful thanks that the Coronation menus are reproduced by gracious permission of Her Majesty Queen Elizabeth II.

It has been pointed out by the Deputy Registrar of the Royal Archives that there would be several official banquets for each Coronation. One did not take place on the actual day of the Coronation, for that would be celebrated by a quieter family dinner.

Details of the recipes for the Coronation dishes are not available so Marguerite Patten has interpreted them as she felt they would have been made.

The Guildhall Menus:

Hamlyn and Marguerite Patten would like to thank the Director of Libraries and Guildhall Art Gallery for permission to reproduce the Jubilee Luncheon menus of George V and Queen Elizabeth II.

Details of the recipes for the Guildhall Menus are not available so Marguerite Patten has interpreted them as she felt they would have been made.

Picture Credits:

Corbis UK Ltd/Hulton Deutsch Collection 74
Hulton Archive endpapers, 2 top left, 2 top right, 2 bottom right, 2 bottom left, 7, 8, 9, 10, 13, 14, 15, 16 right, 17, 18, 19 Top, 20, 21, 22, 23, 24, 25, 38, 41, 42, 43, 45, 46, 47, 48, 49, 50, 51, 65, 66, 67, 76, 77, 78 right, 79, 81, 82, 83, 85, 86, 87, 102, 104, 105, 106 right, 107, 108, 109, 110, 111, 113, 114, 115, 116, 117, 118, 119, 120-121, 121, 122, 135, 139, 141, 142, 144, 145, 146
Robert Opie 1, 3, 5 top, 5 centre left, 5 centre right, 5 bottom, 12, 16 left, 19 bottom, 27, 30, 31, 33, 34, 37, 40, 44, 52, 53, 57, 60, 61, 64, 68, 72, 73, 78 left, 80, 84, 89, 90, 91, 92, 97, 99, 100, 101, 106 left, 112, 124, 127, 128, 130, 133, 136, 140, 147, 149, 150, 154, 156
Rex Features/Tim Rooke 143

Executive Editor Nicola Hill
Editor Abi Rowsell
Senior Designer Joanna Bennett
Designer Bill Mason
Picture Researcher Christine Junemann
Production Controller Lucy Woodhead